Praise for *Relevance*

"Provides an invaluable leadership tool to executives striving to run organizations awash in data and bogged down by mid-level managers 'playing games with numbers' to make their own lives easier—often at the cost of the organization's broader success. A powerful flashlight to help guide the way through the data-overload fog."

—Lew Shuster, CEO, Kemia Inc.

"This is a must-read for any executive involved in developing or executing strategy. It provides a pragmatic framework for setting strategies and for measuring their effectiveness."

—Navneet Govil, controller, Microelectronics Group,
Sun Microsystems, Inc.

"Apgar's ideas will improve business performance because he has thought deeply and critically about the information deluge. Apgar brings the scientific method to information management."

—Chris Flowers, CEO, J.C. Flowers & Co.

"The business world should commend David Apgar for exploring this timely, interesting, and difficult subject."

—Eugene A. Ludwig, founder and CEO,
Promontory Financial Group;
former Comptroller of the Currency (1993–1998)

Relevance

Hitting Your Goals by Knowing What Matters

David Apgar

JOSSEY-BASS
A Wiley Imprint
www.josseybass.com

Published by Jossey-Bass
A Wiley Imprint
989 Market Street, San Francisco, CA 94103-1741—www.josseybass.com

Readers should be aware that Internet Web sites offered as citations and/or sources for further
information may have changed or disappeared between the time this was written and when it
is read.

Limit of Liability/Disclaimer of Warranty: While the publisher and author have used their
best efforts in preparing this book, they make no representations or warranties with respect
to the accuracy or completeness of the contents of this book and specifically disclaim any
implied warranties of merchantability or fitness for a particular purpose. No warranty may
be created or extended by sales representatives or written sales materials. The advice and
strategies contained herein may not be suitable for your situation. You should consult with a
professional where appropriate. Neither the publisher nor author shall be liable for any loss
of profit or any other commercial damages, including but not limited to special, incidental,
consequential, or other damages.

Jossey-Bass books and products are available through most bookstores. To contact Jossey-Bass
directly call our Customer Care Department within the U.S. at 800-956-7739, outside the
U.S. at 317-572-3986, or fax 317-572-4002.

Jossey-Bass also publishes its books in a variety of electronic formats. Some content that
appears in print may not be available in electronic books.

Library of Congress Cataloging-in-Publication Data

Apgar, David.
    Relevance : hitting your goals by knowing what matters/David Apgar.
       p.   cm.
    Includes bibliographical references and index.
    ISBN 978-0-7879-9759-5 (cloth)
      1. Industrial productivity—Measurement. 2. Performance. 3. Benchmarking
    (Management) I. Title.
  HD56.25.A64   2008
  658.4'01—dc22
                                         2007050893

Printed in the United States of America
FIRST EDITION
HB Printing 10 9 8 7 6 5 4 3 2 1

To Phebe Elizabeth and Sarah

Contents

Relevance

Introduction

THE END OF THE INFORMATION REVOLUTION

There was no fog of war over Basra on the seventh day of the invasion of Iraq. Instead of operating in an information vacuum like U.S. Civil War soldiers firing into a smoke-filled field, the American pilots of two A-10 Thunderbolts flying a mission to destroy Iraqi rocket launchers on March 28, 2003, were bathed in a sea of information as dense as the Mesopotamian sunlight. Supporting them were at least three Marine Corps forward air controllers attached to British units on the ground, an AWACS control ship called Sky Chief, a nearby British pilot, and a theater commander called Twin Act.[1]

"Hey, I got a four ship," called POPOV36, one of the A-10 pilots, spotting a suspicious convoy below. "Looks like we got orange panels on them though. Do we have any friendlies up in this area?" Coalition vehicles bore orange panels as markers.

A forward air controller called Manila Hotel checked that the pilot was eight hundred meters north of Basra. "That is an affirm," he replied, affirming a probable target. "You are well clear of friendlies."

"I see multiple riveted vehicles," interjected POPOV35, the other A-10 pilot. "Some look like flatbed trucks and others are green vehicles. Can't quite make out the type. Look like they may be ZIL157s." POPOV36 repeated his sighting of a convoy of four vehicles, the "four ship," for POPOV35's benefit, adding that the vehicles were evenly spaced along a road. POPOV35 replied, "I don't have your visual."

POPOV36 provided more detail to help his wingman find the convoy: "Right underneath you. Right now, there's a canal that

1

runs north/south. There's a small village, and there are vehicles that are spaced evenly there. They look like they have orange panels on though."

POPOV35 reminded him that Manila Hotel said there were no friendly vehicles in the area. "They've got something orange on top of them," pressed POPOV36. "Hey, tell me what type of rocket launchers you got up here?" he asked the air controller. "I think they're rocket launchers." And he added to POPOV35: "Roll up your right wing and look right underneath you."

POPOV35 replied, "I know what you're talking about."

"Okay, well they got orange rockets on them," said POPOV36.

"Orange rockets?" asked POPOV35.

"Yeah, I think so," answered POPOV36. Then he added, "I think killing these damn rocket launchers, it would be great." A minute later he asked POPOV35, "Okay, do you see the orange things on top of them?"

"I'm coming off west," POPOV35 replied. "You roll in. It looks like they are exactly what we're talking about."

"We got visual," said POPOV36. "Okay. I want to get that first one before he gets into town then."

"Get him—get him," urged POPOV35.

"All right, we got rocket launchers, it looks like," said POPOV36.

POPOV36 rolled his A-10 into a vertical dive to strafe what would prove to be a British column, hitting two Scimitar armored vehicles.

This book is about telling in an age of information overload what's relevant to what you're trying to do. The trouble with an overload of information isn't just that it's confusing. It's that the data have conflicting implications. There are no friendly vehicles in the area. But the vehicles below bear something like the coalition's orange marker panels. They could be rocket launchers. But orange is an odd color for a launcher. Our enormous data resources are doing us no favors when they paralyze our decision making. This book helps find what information is most relevant despite the overload.

The transcript from POPOV36's cockpit tape goes on to etch in blood and tears just how futile a surfeit of information can be. Seven seconds after POPOV36 fired again, a second forward air controller, called Lightning34, warned, "Be advised that in the 3122 and 3222 group box you have friendly armor in the area. Yellow, small armored tanks. Just be advised."

A few moments later, a third forward air controller, called Manila 34, ordered: "Hey, POPOV34 [sic], abort your mission. You got a, looks like we might have a blue on blue situation." POPOV35 swore and asked him to confirm they were over friendly vehicles. "Okay, POPOV," called Manila 34. "Just west of the 3–4 easting. On the berm up there, the 3422 area is where we have our friendlies, over."

POPOV35 asked how the friendlies were. Manila 34 told them they were getting an initial brief that one was killed and one wounded. "I'm going to be sick," said POPOV35. A few moments later, he made the comment to his fellow pilot that lit up newspaper accounts of the incident: "We're in jail dude."

"Relaying for TWINACT," broadcast Sky Chief, "the A-10s are running against friendlies."

A British pilot repeated: "POPOV35, this is COSTA58. Relaying message for TWINACT. Abort. Abort."

Of course, the two pilots had already aborted their mission. Their curses ran from denial to anger to grief. "They did say there were no friendlies," moaned POPOV35.

And as Lance Corporal of Horse Matt Hull, a young Englishman from Windsor, Berkshire, just short of his twenty-sixth birthday, died below, POPOV36 wept.

Dimensions of an Information Crisis

The information revolution is drawing to a close as our expanding information resources bury decisions under ever higher piles of conflicting data. The next section blames this on our neglect of relevance as raw data get cheaper to generate. The third section asks how we can learn from experience despite the glut of information and explains why I want to address this challenge by focusing specifically on performance experience—on the results of our projects, businesses, and ventures. The fourth section summarizes this book's answer to the challenge of learning from the reams of performance data our organizations collect. It calls for the development of performance strategies explicit enough to be testable, the derivation of performance metrics from the assumptions behind those strategies, and the use of performance results to reveal errors in our strategic goals and assumptions, as well as execution. This section outlines the dimensions of the problem.

The sources of evidence for an information crisis provide a decent list of people who should consider reading this book. One group it excludes would be all of those whose e-mail inboxes, performance scorecards, operating dashboards, and management reports are growing shorter. If your organization is asking you to cope with less information, these pages may not speak to you. Those feeling oppressed by operating data should read on.

Small business owners and general managers of the divisions of larger firms may suffer most. They often feel they have to monitor everything that could possibly go wrong in their organizations. If that's not bad enough, the general managers also have to watch the metrics their CEOs monitor—even if those metrics are irrelevant to their plans. This book proposes a three-part program to determine which metrics really matter.

It confronts the core challenge before finance professionals—including chief financial officers, controllers, divisional finance directors, audit directors, and financial analysts—of reporting financial information to improve performance without overwhelming their organization. The book's tools will also help human resource executives design performance goals to develop high-potential staff. And it addresses the increasingly intense performance assessment demands on information technology groups reflected in the proliferation of project management offices.

The book's answers to the learning challenge posed by exponential information growth are directly relevant to military organizations as they struggle to simplify the information cascading down on combat theater teams and rethink that information in terms of conflict between opposing networks—so-called net-centric warfare. Nondefense government officials are in equal need of ways to focus on what, of all the information at their disposal, really matters to policy plans and proposals.

Ironically it may be nongovernmental organizations that have undergone the biggest change in their use of performance data over the past five years. Impact assessment groups have stepped up efforts at the World Bank, the International Monetary Fund, and their sister institutions under the International Bank for Reconstruction and Development. Charities like the Gates Foundation, moreover, are applying fast-to-fail performance criteria to their initiatives to promote learning as well as husband resources. The growing focus on performance evaluation in a context of complex and often conflicting objectives is sharpening these organizations' appetite for a robust framework like this book's approach to strategic goals, assumptions, and success indicators.

The most dramatic development in performance assessment over the past decade, however, has been the effort to integrate functional measures for marketing, research and development, procurement, supply chain planning, process improvement, quality control, sales, and customer service into a coherent view of corporate effectiveness. Often taking advantage of enterprise resource planning systems, this effort has evolved in two directions. Numerically intensive continuous process improvement programs, usually found at larger manufacturers, tend to require heavy levels of up-front investment. Qualitative approaches like balanced scorecards are a little less expensive but often grow complex without measurable benefits. This book proposes an approach to defining and measuring performance that applies the discipline of continuous process improvement to strategy evaluation and development without disrupting existing systems or processes.

One could easily go beyond these examples of information overloads in organizations to list the kinds of financial, consumer, and legal information that bombard us in our personal lives and complicate our decisions about careers, spending, investment, households, and even networks of friends and relatives. The problem is familiar and pervasive. In fact, it's woven into the texture of contemporary life tightly enough to mark a period in the very information revolution that gave rise to it.

Relevance and the End of the Information Revolution

It's one thing to say our information resources are burying decisions under ever-higher piles of conflicting data, but it's quite another to declare an end to the information revolution. Even so, I think our neglect of relevance in information—encouraged by the availability of raw data that keep getting cheaper to generate—has drawn a curtain on it.

A major idea in this book is that the usefulness of any piece of information depends on two complementary values: its specificity—which you can think of as its content, or simply how surprising it is—and its relevance. Specificity gives you a sense of the power of a piece of information because you can draw more conclusions from precise outcomes than from vague ones. A result reflecting one out of ten possibilities, for example, tells you more than a result reflecting one out of just two.

Relevance complements specificity. While specificity is intrinsic to information—it's the same no matter what your goal is—relevance depends entirely on that goal, or at least on the assumptions behind it. As I use the term in this book, *relevance* has to do with how well a piece of information tests your expectations.

It's fairly clear that both specificity and relevance are important in evaluating information. The startling part of the idea is that they complement each other—they're all that matters. It's startling but plausible. To see how specificity and relevance fit together, imagine you're throwing paintballs at a target. Specificity is like the size of the paintballs. Big ones resemble unspecific results; they don't gauge your accuracy. Relevance is more like their shape. Round ones that stay intact until they hit the target—like relevant information—really test your aim. Those that scatter or leave thin, oblong marks do not. To improve your aim, you need balls that leave precise round marks—information that's both specific and relevant.

The idea that specificity and relevance drive the value of information helps explain how the information revolution's economics may have undermined it. Technologies like microprocessors and optical fiber have basically cut the cost of specificity. Whether you run a division, compile financial reports, or manage service operations, you've been able to get more data faster. The relevance of those data has mattered less and less because increasingly you've been able to compensate with volume. And as we've grown used to less relevant data, I suspect that we've formed two bad habits.

The first bad habit is *requirements-based analysis*. Instead of devising a specific strategy to meet a financial goal like a sales or profit target, we're increasingly tempted to enumerate requirements for meeting the goal. Requirements might include minimum levels of staffing, funding, technology functionality, or process performance. Budget planning increasingly follows this course, working backward from profit targets to sales requirements and cost ceilings. And executives tend to use balanced scorecards, one of the most widespread management tools, as menus of common requirements.[2]

In this book, I liken these necessary conditions for meeting a goal to lists of ingredients. The comparison helps explain the appeal of requirements; it's as easy to find metrics for them as it is to determine whether you have all the required ingredients for the dish you're cooking for dinner. But just as you can know all the ingredients for a dish without having a recipe for it, you can meet every conceivable requirement for a goal without knowing how to achieve it. Simply put, requirements are not strategies. And unlike strategies, there's little to learn when they fail to work. That may be another key to their appeal: you can be right about requirements even if a goal proves elusive. And it leads to the second bad habit: our growing reliance on *red herrings*.

Red herrings are results that appear to confirm your plans but in reality are merely consistent with them. You might think customers will prefer cell phones with Internet browsers, for example, and find they purchase more of a model that includes them. But if that model is also much easier to use than its predecessors, the increase in customer uptake may be a red herring as far as your assumption about browsers is concerned. The new model's results, in other words, are not necessarily relevant to expectations about cell phone browsers.

As our enterprise planning systems accumulate more and more data of limited relevance to our plans, red herrings are bound to proliferate. That's fine as long as you recognize them. The trouble is that you may think they confirm your strategy. Worse, you may be tempted to build a strategy largely out of requirements and rely on irrelevant metrics—on red herrings—to test its more explicit prescriptions. Experience won't teach you much about such a strategy: events are unlikely to prove the requirements wrong, and the red herrings are unlikely to challenge the explicit prescriptions.

Our declining ability to learn from experience as we accumulate conflicting data marks the end of the information revolution. Hastening its close is a characteristic style of performance analysis that I call the *analyze-execute system*. It has three tenets: you can reduce any account of performance to a set of basic facts, those facts imply a correct strategy, and so finding the right strategy reduces to collecting enough facts. These tenets contradict the way we formulate and test hypotheses in our conduct of science—scientists rarely just collect facts—and yet we embrace them in business and government.

Why do we do that? Perhaps it's not just that we want to be right—which is less likely if you lay out explicit strategies that events might prove wrong and track highly relevant metrics that will tell you as soon as they do. Perhaps it's that we hope we've hit on an objective way of looking at our businesses and the world around us that captures the way they really are. We distrust the filter of our point of view.

But the question remains: Why do we want to be right in such a metaphysical way rather than just achieving a goal? The philosopher Richard Rorty offered the controversial explanation that we pursue a kind of objectivity beyond mere public evaluation because we fear we'll be forgotten. He wrote, "The picture of a common human nature oriented towards correspondence to reality as it is in itself comforts us with the thought that even if our civilization is destroyed, even if all memory of our political or intellectual or artistic community is erased, the race is fated to recapture the virtues and the insights and the achievements which were the glory of that community."[3]

Rorty may have put his finger on a profound reason that we're not content with making up business strategies and testing them for errors. Perhaps we really do crave insights and business strategies that not only work but are somehow true for all time and in all languages. There's a big practical advantage, however, to my proposal that cheap information has tempted us to neglect relevance and led us into some bad habits. It means you may not have to develop a view on the fate of the world to learn from experience despite the information overload our organizations produce. Paying close attention to relevance may be enough.

Why Focus on Performance Management?

If it's true that the information revolution has generated piles of data so complex we can hardly tell what matters, how are we to learn from experience going forward? Of course, broad questions like this invite answers so broad that they never get around to concrete suggestions. But a narrower question could fail to do justice to all the ways information overloads hamper decisions we need to make in everyday life. For this book, I thought the best bet was to investigate a specific problem that raises the full spectrum of challenges posed by information gluts and try to provide an explicit solution.

It's probably no surprise that a business writer would identify a core problem in business learning—selecting the best performance indicators to accelerate it and shape our organizational strategies—as the most revealing way to address the phenomenon of information overload. I suspect many business readers will grant me the benefit of the doubt on this. Here I'll try to persuade the nonbusiness reader that the challenge of learning from an organization's performance experience uniquely illuminates the broader question of what really matters in the sea of information around us.

One reason is that organizations—and businesses in particular—are awash in a rich mix of information. Businesses were the earliest investors in information technology so they can gather a lot of data. They're under competitive pressure to figure out what works, so they collect information on factors like work effort and resources, as well as on results like profit. And they collect it frequently to speed up decisions. As a result, the performance reports businesses produce are especially rich in data with conflicting implications. That makes them a good model for the mixed signals that create so much confusion in our increasingly information-intensive daily lives.

The other reason is that while any solution to the information overload in business organizations may be more structured than we need for solving the kinds of personal problems that arise in career choice and managing busy households, that very structure should clarify principles for simplifying our lives. For example, the testable strategies, assumption-based indicators, and critical strategy reviews that I propose in this book also serve as models for precision in our personal expectations, milestones for testing those expectations, and realism about changing them in the light of experience. The principles for determining what matters in the performance experience of a business are clear and structured versions of those that can determine what matters in our own experience.

Before going on to a summary of the book's solution to the problem of organizational learning in the face of overwhelming and conflicting performance data, here are twelve questions that it should help you answer. The Conclusion takes a stab at summarizing the answers developed across its chapters:

1. How is organizational learning related to growth?
2. What's wrong with balanced scorecards, and what's the alternative?
3. How should we set performance goals?
4. How do testable strategies help us learn from experience?
5. Which metrics matter?
6. How can we measure relevance?
7. What kinds of acquisitions are relevant to our business?
8. Are forecasts necessary?
9. Why do traditional performance reviews destroy morale?
10. What's the relation between performance volatility and compensation?
11. What does relevance have to do with leadership?
12. What's a relevance revolution?

Relearning Learning from Experience

This book argues that learning from experience—when you're confronting too much of it—requires three things: the development of performance strategies explicit enough to be testable, the derivation of performance indicators from the assumptions behind those strategies, and the use of performance results to reveal errors in goals and assumptions as well as execution. Chapters One and Two deal with testable strategies, Chapters Three and Four deal with assumption-based metrics, and Chapters Five and Six deal with strategy reviews.

Chapter One uses a cautionary tale from BP and examples from Alcoa and GE to argue that learning from experience requires performance strategies explicit enough to be testable. A strategy is testable if it spells out goals and assumptions about how to achieve them that could conceivably prove wrong. Chapter Two proposes *eight-line strategies* for distilling the strategy relevant to a manager at any level of an organization to a short list of testable assumptions. These strategies are basically devices to help you identify the key unsettled assumptions or biggest bets you're making when you project a result. Laying the foundation for vastly simplified management reporting and performance reviews, these assumptions let you pick out the facts most relevant to your strategy from large amounts of conflicting performance data.

To learn from experience despite the noise of that conflicting data, Chapter Three derives performance indicators from key strategic assumptions—and not from balanced lists of output targets and input requirements. It draws examples from Media General, Saatchi & Saatchi, and Ingersoll-Rand—three companies that participated in Kaplan's and Norton's Balanced Scorecard Collaborative—to show that however important it may be to balance short- and long-term concerns, the pursuit of balance in what we measure reflects confusion about why we measure it.

Chapter Four helps you select a handful of critical performance indicators by defining their relevance with respect to your assumptions about what will achieve a strategy's goals. A performance indicator is relevant to a strategic assumption, according to the definition, if the assumption's truth or falsity greatly affects the results you expect. This definition marries aspects of Bayesian probability, which tracks how new evidence affects beliefs, and information theory, which basically measures what we don't know, to avoid false conclusions and mimics the skeptical use of performance data at Toyota and Capital One.

Requiring only a pen and piece of paper, a tool called the *metrics matrix* uses the definition to determine which indicators best test each of your key assumptions from an eight-line strategy.

The handful of resulting indicators are the only ones you need to track until your strategy changes. Balanced scorecards, in contrast, rarely test strategies. They have a natural tendency to test something quite different: requirements for success. The problem is that you can meet a list of requirements and still miss the goal. Since there is no end to the requirements you can identify, balanced scorecards tend to accumulate more and more metrics without ever defining a testable strategy.

To learn from increasingly complex experience, finally, we must use performance results to reveal errors in our goals and assumptions, as well as execution. Splitting the difference between actual and expected performance results into execution, uncontrollable, and strategy gaps, Chapter Five proposes a model *strategy review* that explicitly challenges strategic plans and assumptions in place of traditional reviews of performance results that focus only on execution. Strategy reviews look at every performance period as a controlled experiment. These experiments naturally test work effort and risk forecasts, but they also test the quality of the assumptions relating that effort and those forecasts to results. The biggest benefit of strategy reviews is motivational because organizations that don't look systematically for strategy errors in their performance results force their operating managers to protect themselves from being blamed for missing unrealistic goals.

Our organizations won't sustain growth, Chapter Six argues further, unless we use the pattern of gaps in our performance results to review strategy and revise tactics continuously. Nestlé provides a powerful example of a performance system that can telescope the review of that pattern into a single performance period. The pattern compresses your organization's performance experience into three numbers. By telling you whether your assumptions about execution, risk, or strategy are most in need of repair, the pattern of gaps lets you allocate scarce talent to your most persistent problems. The result is a fully engaged management team that evolves strategy continuously by testing and revising assumptions at every level of the organization.

Taken together, the testable strategies, assumption-based metrics, and strategy reviews proposed here turn traditional planning and performance systems inside out, basing them on your biggest bets about how to achieve a goal. These bets are more like recipes than lists of ingredients. They specify how to achieve an objective, may be wrong, and require testing and revision. But they focus you on the performance results from which you can learn the most—about your current strategy.

Call this alternative performance system the *guess-test system*—in contrast to analyze-execute systems that try to derive strategy from the raw data of a comprehensive scorecard and test only whether execution is faithful to it. While guesses in the form of assumptions may seem like a strange place to start learning from experience, the discipline of testing strategy rapidly hones them to the realities of your business.

The Larger Relevance of Relevance

The *Washington Post*'s Steven Pearlstein once complained to me that books offering business advice too often claim their frameworks solve every problem known to humans. This is the section where I run the risk of doing exactly that. But before I do, here are a few thoughts on what this book is not and what I think books like it should try to accomplish.

It's not a book of academic case studies, even though it provides plenty of business examples, opinionated accounts of developments at well-known companies, and nonbusiness examples as well. I think books laying out a potentially controversial argument like this one make a mistake if they try to prove their point with detailed case studies. The selection of details can easily make a case appear to support an argument that it actually undermines. The examples here are illustrations, not proofs.

Business books advancing new or neglected claims also need to offer advice that every reader could, in principle, follow. If that advice is to collect the most data, for example, those who follow it will conflict with one another and may be better off ignoring it. That's not a limitation of the advice on these pages because it shows you how to find information relevant to your own assumptions. If your assumptions are creative, the book's implications for you will be unique. This is not a zero-sum book.

Nor will the advice in this book restore organizational morale, separate good mergers from bad ones, calculate optimal compensation levels, solve complex environmental threats, or identify great leaders. And yet its themes touch on all of these things. It's worth mentioning the connections as a reminder that the deepest problems in our businesses, organizations, and institutions echo larger problems in public life.

Relevance bears strongly on organizational morale. The reason is that performance indicators selected for their relevance to strategic assumptions will naturally evaluate the quality of plans as well as the quality of effort against them. And that's all you may need to rescue the morale of a division chafing under goals the staff feel they can't control—a clear understanding that strategies and goals are subject to criticism in the light of performance results as well as execution. Without such an understanding, the staff may feel they're being held responsible for someone else's planning errors.

Acquisition targets that are relevant to your business are good; others aren't. But there may be a deeper connection between relevance and acquisition planning. This book's definition of relevance provides a criterion for determining when the ongoing business results and experience of an acquisition candidate can help improve the strategy of your business. And that kind of cross-fertilization may be more important than cost synergies at a time when technology, outsourcing, and provider networks can help almost any scale of business reach world-class levels of operating efficiency.

Relevance and compensation are also related. Variability in the results of metrics relevant to core strategic assumptions reveals a lot about the volatility of your business environment. So it also reveals a lot about the difficulty of the business problems you must solve. Under the right conditions, you can use that variability to make sure the difficulty of the jobs of similarly paid executives is comparable and compensation is fair.

Relevance even bears on complex problems like global warming and economic development. A primary reason for the complexity of these problems is the sheer difficulty of measuring the success of alternative environmental and development strategies. Both areas cry out for hard thought on how to find metrics that test what these strategies really assume. This book tries to supply some of that hard thought. But its larger public policy contribution may be to encourage a more experimental approach to problems of public choice. For example, the belief that our latest development theories were right and lacked only confirmation has prevented us from making headway on development problems for decades. It's time to try assuming that we're wrong.

Finally, relevance helps separate leadership traits such as resolve and flexibility from stubbornness and inconstancy. There are as many dramatic cases of CEOs who persevered and succeeded, for instance, as CEOs who sank with their ships. It may be easier to draw the line if we recognize that learning from experience requires leaders to be clear about their ideas precisely in order to subject them to the harshest relevant tests.

What these connections really suggest is that the testable strategies, relevant metrics, and reviews of results proposed in the following pages are more than a guide for coping with performance information overload. They embody an experimental approach to management and problem solving. It's an approach that reflects a thorough fallibilism about the strategies we construct to meet our goals and an optimism that we can always do better.

It may be too much to hope this approach spares the life of a future Matt Hull. But the A-10 cockpit transcript shows that even in the heat of battle, it's possible to ask what we're really assuming. And from there it's a short step to focusing on what could prove us wrong rather than just what suggests we may be right.

1

GROWING TO LEARN

As the 2006 war between Israel and Lebanon staggered toward a U.N.-brokered cease-fire, the Iraq war spun into sectarian conflict, and oil prices floated over seventy-five dollars a barrel, BP (once British Petroleum) revealed it was shutting down operations in Prudhoe Bay, Alaska—about 8 percent of U.S. petroleum production capacity. The Organization of Petroleum Exporting Countries eagerly announced it would make up any shortfall.

BP admitted it had not checked some of its North Slope transit pipelines since it ran a "smart pig" corrosion-sensing device through them in 1992. "With hindsight, that's clearly a gap in our program," acknowledged BP corrosion management and chemicals program team leader Bill Hedges.[1] Ignoring the reliability of the pipes carrying 8 percent of U.S. petroleum production is quite a gap. By the same token, you might say forgetting about the Russian winter was a gap in Napoleon's program.

Of course, bad things happen to good people. But BP's run of bad news in 2005 and 2006 started to look systematic. The shutdown occurred five months after an earlier leak from one of the company's Alaska pipelines went undetected and dumped 200,000 gallons of oil on the North Slope.[2] And in June 2006, the Commodity Futures Trading Commission accused BP of rigging the propane market in February 2004.[3] After substantial forward propane purchases—contracts requiring other parties to deliver the fuel at a fixed price in the future—BP allegedly withheld its own refined propane from the market to create an artificial scarcity. That any trader would risk BP's reputation for the caper's paltry $20 million reported yield is astonishing.

The context of these missteps is the real issue, however. Two of them followed an explosion at the firm's Texas City refinery that killed fifteen and injured one hundred in March 2005. The Occupational Safety and Health Organization fined BP $21 million for "egregious, willful violations of safety standards."[4] The U.S. Chemical Safety and Hazard Investigation Board preliminarily determined in October 2006 that faulty equipment and staff reductions were responsible for the tragedy.[5]

If ever a tragedy put a company on notice to lock down its operations, you would think the worst U.S. industrial accident in a decade would do it. Why didn't BP's extraction businesses respond to the terrible experience of its refining businesses?

This chapter argues that learning from experience requires performance strategies explicit enough to be testable. A strategy is testable if it spells out goals and assumptions about how to achieve them that could conceivably prove wrong. You might ask why learning from experience has anything to do with the strategy you're pursuing. The chapter claims that what you learn depends on what you expect, which is what a testable performance strategy lays out. For example, BP's failure to learn from repeated mistakes in its American operations followed an initiative that devolved strategy setting to operating units. The first section of the chapter argues that the lack of testable clarity in BP's strategies impaired its ability to learn and adapt.

This is important because BP is hardly alone in devolving strategy to independent business units. In fact, the failure to lay out testable strategies is widespread. It afflicts any organization that pursues stagnant or chaotic strategies, including both those with slow-to-mature "hockey stick" profit goals that are impossible to test in the short run (think of profit projections that run flat for three years and suddenly jump up in the fourth) and those that derive their goals from investor requirements without specifying any operating assumptions. The second section of the chapter contends that strategy clear enough to test is extraordinarily rare. That rarity explains the growing difficulty of determining what matters in our voluminous performance reports.

The third section of the chapter shows how setting testable strategies helps firms learn from experience. Alcoa and GE both manage themselves by laying out clear, changing performance goals and strategic assumptions that they regularly put to the test. The section draws links between this practice, Rand Corporation's assumption-based planning, and Rita McGrath's and Ian MacMillan's discovery-driven planning.

Chapter Two continues the argument by proposing a method called *eight-line strategies* for distilling the strategy relevant to a manager at any level of a firm to a short list of testable assumptions. Setting out a testable strategy is the first step in what I call the *guess-test* system of performance management. Starting with guesses in the form of testable strategies, this system lets you pick out facts that can improve decisions from piles of conflicting performance data. In essence, it uses performance results as a means of sharpening strategy continuously and not just of tracking execution.

Accountability at the Expense of Firmwide Learning at BP

BP is a good example of this chapter's theme that lack of testable clarity in a company's strategy can impair its ability to learn and adapt. The run of accidents and scandals in BP's American operations constituted a firmwide learning failure, and the setbacks followed an initiative that devolved strategy setting to operating units.

The learning failure is well documented. "It is a very significant finding that BP does not effectively investigate incidents throughout the corporation," warns U.S. Chemical Safety Board spokesman Daniel Horowitz. "If you're not learning from near misses, you're not in a position to prevent major disasters like the one in Texas City."[6] What impeded learning at BP?

The company underwent an organizational change starting in 1995 large enough to account for its uncharacteristic swerve into a series of apparently systematic mistakes a decade later. As John Roberts tells it in *The Modern Firm,* the company reduced staff in its corporate headquarters by 80 percent under CEO Robert Horton's "Project 1990."[7] At the same time, the upstream business cluster BP Exploration devolved strategy to its business units in a disaggregated model called "asset federation." After leading BP Exploration's transformation, John Browne became Group CEO in 1995.[8]

That transformation transferred responsibility for performance down to the managers of forty individual sites or fields from the regional operating companies that had previously run them. Browne eliminated the regional operating companies, cut back the management of BP Exploration to an executive committee of himself and two others, and transferred key technical staff to the fields.[9]

Managers of the fields and other assets started to sign performance contracts with Browne's executive committee. The contracts held them responsible for production volumes and expenditures but left them "empowered to figure out how to achieve their promised performance. They could decide on outsourcing and choose suppliers, do their own hiring, and determine where and how to drill."[10]

Institutional memory and learning are at risk in this sort of disaggregated organizational design. In fact, Roberts makes the point that any organizational design trades off initiative—maximized under Browne's plan—and cooperation—for which, like institutional learning, Browne's system needed to find other solutions. "But the changes," he writes of Browne's design, "also created a great need for the business units to cooperate in sharing best practice and in supporting one another in solving technical and commercial problems—activities that were previously handled by the center, but that it now lacked the resources to undertake."[11]

To fill this need, BP Exploration created a system of "peer assists" by which a unit could call on any other unit in its group of peers (defined as those with assets at a similar life stage) for help with commercial and technological problems. The delegation of responsibility for performance to individual asset units, supported by the system of peer assists, proved so successful in streamlining operations and cutting costs that Browne implemented it across the entire company when he became Group CEO.[12]

The groups of similar asset-based business units that facilitated peer assists also facilitated "peer challenges." In a peer challenge, a business unit questions the performance goals another unit has negotiated with the executive committee.[13] A peer group's collective responsibility for meeting each member unit's goals and for allocating resources among the members is supposed to motivate thoughtful challenges.

Neither peer assists nor challenges, however, were enough to prevent calamity. In investigating the Texas City explosion, a panel headed by James Baker found that workers at a sister refinery in Whiting, Indiana, reported that "preventive maintenance was seldom practiced, the refinery had a 'run until it breaks' mentality, and the workforce had a great deal of experience running equipment with 'Band-Aids.' "[14] In other words, the Whiting plant ran under conditions like those at Texas City. Peer assists failed the two refineries in that they did not usefully pool their experience. And peer challenges failed them in that lax safety and upkeep practices prevailed despite worker concerns.

BP's system of independent business unit strategy setting combined with peer challenges failed to produce uniformly explicit, testable strategies when it came to performance sustainability. Insofar as peer challenges brought objective scrutiny to bear on performance goals, they were a brilliant innovation. They nevertheless have two disadvantages from the perspective of organizational learning. Their resource implications introduce an element of competition among peer group units that can undermine peer-to-peer learning. At the same time, patterns of cooperative laxity can emerge that weaken the search for continuous improvements.

These two disadvantages may seem contradictory, but both are often on display in the behavior of boards of directors. For example, CEOs who sit on boards compete with one another informally for the honors that go with top pay from their own companies. The record of these boards, however, as rehearsed in literally hundreds of studies, reports, and articles, has been one of at least equal informal collaboration to relax CEO pay package discipline.[15] So competition and collaboration can go hand in hand.

Board behavior shows why BP should not have relied on peer challenges to drive its field managers to learn from one another's experience. Small peer groups don't consistently raise the stringency of one another's performance goals because cooperative leniency keeps breaking out. Even without explicit cooperation, you can always find out by trial and error which of your peers tend to reciprocate when you give them the benefit of doubt on a lenient goal. Over time, lenience becomes the norm.

BP's system of independent business unit strategy setting combined with peer challenges also failed to produce uniformly explicit, testable strategies when it came to risk management. The manager of a business unit will question peer levels of operating risks less closely than a corporate center risk manager will, if only because individual units experience mishaps less frequently than peer groups as a whole. For example, if a group of ten similar operating units experiences one major mishap every ten years and one early warning sign every year, then each operating unit will experience a major mishap only once a century on average and an early warning sign only once a decade. A central planner for any group of units will try to aggregate their risk experience and expose her individual managers to it. But the delegation of strategy review to operating units may reduce managers' sensitivity to the group's catastrophic risks because individual units can run so long without seeing any evidence of them at all.

Something may seem jarring about the proposition that BP's delegation of strategy setting to operating units impaired their ability to learn from experience and adapt to changing conditions. Surely Browne had adaptation foremost in mind when he gave the managers of individual operating assets more responsibility for how they met their goals. You can't blame a corporate learning failure on an organizational innovation that moves decisions closer to the people with the information to make them.

The answer to the conundrum may be that Browne's was an incomplete revolution. He may well have been right that BP's operating units—or at least its upstream units in exploration and production—could operate independently. If so, they may prove most valuable under independent ownership. The parts of BP Exploration may someday prove more valuable than the whole.

The reason stems from the very weakness of running completely independent extraction operations. A stand-alone operation's lack of resilience after major mishaps heightens its managers' sensitivity to any kind of latent risk. Independent operating units have to learn from a narrow base of business experience, but they may compensate with a heightened appetite for relevant outside information. Operating units that can fall back on the financial strength of a firm like BP have access to more useful peer information on risks but less incentive to scrutinize it.

We may never know whether John Browne was right. He was committed to his management revolution at BP but did not take its Texas City tragedy and other setbacks lightly. He is the type of systematic thinker who might even have considered the radical step of divestitures. But he resigned on January 12, 2007, earlier than he had planned.

The idea that businesses that don't benefit from strategy coordination should be independent raises a broader theme explored in this book. According to classical industrial economics, the cost of doing business defines the natural scope of a company. The example of BP suggests this may be wrong. The mutual relevance of the various activities of a business may define its natural scope instead.

The classic idea that transaction costs determine the natural scope of a firm follows from an argument of British Nobel prize winner and University of Chicago professor Ronald Coase. He claimed that a market with clear property rights will produce the same efficient outcome no matter who owns the property unless there are high transaction costs in the market.[16]

For example, it should be just as efficient for two business activities to trade supplies within a single firm as it is for a similar pair of activities in separate firms to trade supplies—so long as transaction costs are low. When transaction costs are high, however, it may be more efficient to keep the two business activities within a single firm. In this case, the firm may be able to cut the cost of the activities by mandating the terms of their interactions and exchanges.

This section provides a reason for thinking that high transaction costs are a special case of situations where companies can coordinate activities more efficiently than markets can. It suggests companies may coordinate activities more efficiently than markets when the results of one activity are relevant to the plans of another, regardless of transaction costs. The case where one business unit's experience applies strongly to the management of another unit's risks is an example. More than internal transaction costs, the mutual relevance of divisions' results may shape the modern firm.

The Rarity of Strategic Clarity

It may seem surprising that a company like BP could have failed to lay out group strategies clearly enough to tell from experience which parts worked and which parts did not. But strategies clear enough to test are extraordinarily rare. Clarity is the victim any time an organization pursues *stagnant* or *chaotic* strategies. Stagnant strategies include the hockey-stick projections in naively optimistic venture capital presentations because they are impossible to test in the short run. Typical examples of chaotic strategies are goals derived from investor requirements that don't specify operating assumptions. The rarity of strategic clarity helps explain why it's so hard to tell what matters in our burgeoning performance reports.

The failure to lay out testable strategies is widespread. A strategy is testable if it spells out goals and assumptions about how to achieve them that could conceivably prove wrong. A strategy could prove wrong if the performance results of an organization pursuing it are capable at least in principle of revealing its flaws. It's hard to imagine what, for instance, could count against the vague strategy to increase sales by hiring more salespeople. But results could well refute the clearer strategy of increasing sales 20 percent by hiring 10 percent more sales staff. What makes such a strategy clear—or at least clear enough to test—is the possibility of showing it's not quite right.

In some ways, this kind of clarity is a low bar. Plenty of strategies are clear in this sense and yet still not advisable. Even so, clear strategies are few and far between. For example, both chaotic and stagnant strategies fail to clear the clarity bar. And yet most strategies, as we'll see, fall into one of these two categories.

Stagnant Strategies

Stagnant strategies are unclear the way habits are unclear. Habits get things done, but it's usually not clear how well. We may as a matter of habit get through all seventy e-mails we receive every day, for example, but it's not clear we do it efficiently and it's not clear which of our e-mail habits are particularly effective. We set no expectations for getting through those e-mails, so we don't look for better ways to process them.

Strategies often become stagnant because their goals are stagnant. Such strategies may suffice to meet their flat-line goals. But since it's not clear by how wide a margin they should meet those goals, just passing doesn't really tell you much about them. A great example is the notorious hockey-stick graph endemic to project plans and new business proposals that forecasts a great long-term gain after a string of break-even years. It's a warning sign of a strategy free to stagnate until the curve finally turns up. Hockey-stick projections are supposed to clinch business cases for new initiatives, but they really say, "Trust me." They offer no way to test a strategy to see whether it's working until the end of the forecast period—usually too late.

Readers who, like me, may have used a hockey-stick projection or two in a moment of weakness in the past will be tempted to protest that these projections at least allow long-term thinking and planning. Some ideas take a long time to bear fruit, goes the argument. But since all of our financial reporting focuses on quarterly results, it militates against the very long-term plans we may most need. The least we can do is to allow our best new initiatives enough time to gestate.

The problem with this defense of long-term goals is that it affords no way to tell exactly which one really is your best new initiative. Calling an initiative a best bet is, after all, a theory. And theories are worthless if there's no way to test them. To see whether one of several possible initiatives really is most promising, you need to devise some near-term indicator that it's working. Such an indicator lets you test and adapt the strategy behind the initiative. It keeps the strategy from stagnating until the time that the upswing in a hockey-stick projection eventually puts it to the test.

If lax and static goals really do allow strategies to become stagnant, there may be more to the pursuit of aggressive growth goals than wishful thinking and willful ignorance of the law of averages. To meet high-growth goals, according to this view, means more than to win at the expense of competitors. It means that the organization pursuing those goals is continually testing its strategy and sensing change. Instead of saying organizations must learn in order to grow—following Nelson and Winter, who called growth a process of pure selection when they launched evolutionary economics in 1982—it may be truer to say that organizations must grow to learn.[17]

Chaotic Strategies

Chaotic strategies, in contrast, are unclear because they're too fragmented or volatile to attribute results to any one aspect of them. Several years ago, for example, I asked my staff in the Corporate Executive Board's subscription-based research program for treasurers to do the following in a single fiscal year: develop a new online bank credit tool; segment the program's market according to capital structure; analyze our marketing success with each segment; emphasize the most enthusiastic segments in scheduling marketing calls; make quarterly checkup calls on each member; analyze treasurers' business processes; and reorganize our content offerings in terms of the treasury processes that each offering supported.

This, it's embarrassing to realize, is a good example of a chaotic strategy. It contains seven new initiatives, reflecting seven ways the program's prior strategy might have been wrong about how the business should really work. Moreover, the initiatives struck out in different directions. The multiplicity and incoherence of the initiatives made it hard to tell at the end of the year which ones to keep and which to adjust. Would slow sales, for example, mean that the bank credit tool underperformed or was hard to explain; that the market segmentation missed the market's real fault lines; that the segment analysis drew mistaken conclusions; that call schedulers had placed prospects in the wrong segments; that our treasury business process analysis was wrong; or that our content reorganization was opaque? Would disappointing current subscriber renewals mean any of these or, alternatively, that checkup call execution was poor?

This kind of chaotic strategy is common because it's a natural response to a tough goal or an urgent need to close a challenging performance gap. In these situations, there is a strong temptation to make lots of changes and "let a thousand flowers bloom." The advantage of such an energetic response is that it increases the likelihood that at least one of the changes you make will actually improve results. The disadvantage, characteristic of all chaotic strategies or chaotic strategic shifts, is that you won't know what worked.

Chaotic strategies also include those derived by reasoning backward from investor requirements—without specifying the operating assumptions behind the reasoning. Many companies derive their budgets this way, determining how much profit each unit must contribute to meet a promise to the market. But unless such a strategy lays out how to achieve its goals, there's no way to tell what went wrong if it misses them.

Even planning systems designed to generate testable strategies fall into this trap. For example, the reverse income statements in Rita McGrath's and Ian MacMillan's discovery-driven planning, described in the next section, work back from a profit target to generate the line items of an income statement that would hit it.[18] These line items might include segment revenue, direct costs, and indirect costs. They're supposed to suggest the key assumptions of a testable strategy, but they don't tell you how to hit the strategy's target. There might be hundreds of ways to do so—all consistent with the line item requirements.

More broadly, finance executives are increasingly adopting versions of aspiration-based planning to focus their efforts to improve operating decisions. The idea is to ask operating managers where they hope to take their divisions in three or five years—their aspirations. The next step is to assess gaps between current capabilities and what those aspirations require. Some finance teams are even gearing up to fill those gaps.

Aspiration-based planning lends itself to capability analysis, but it doesn't necessarily generate testable strategies. It may elicit admirably clear and ambitious goals. And it may not be hard to derive requirements from those goals. But even if you meet every requirement you can imagine, you may not hit a goal. Requirements are much broader than specific prescriptions for achieving a goal. That's why requirements are relatively easy to list, while testable strategies can be fiendishly hard to devise. For example, it's obvious that you have to schedule at least ten visits with prospective customers to have a hope of selling ten insurance policies. That's a requirement. But scheduling those visits hardly guarantees the sales. A sales strategy requires more knowledge, such as research into your prospects' needs. We'll return to the sharp distinction between requirements and strategies in Chapter Three.

Strategies that specify a final goal but not how to achieve it resemble those that strike out in too many directions at once. Both kinds of strategy may have stringent goals, but neither helps you find out from experience what achieves them.

Whether an organization's strategy is chaotic because it specifies too many new activities or none, its marching orders boil down to scrambling. Often that's all you can do when you have a target you must meet in any way you can. But it's hard to learn what works in a chaotic scramble to hit a target. And if you face a competitor who, instead of scrambling, can test alternative means for achieving his goals, you'll learn more slowly.

This may be why so many venture capitalists bring in managers with clear, simple plans to turn around start-ups that founders have made frantic in a never-ending scramble to meet investor targets. There's nothing wrong with the joyous frenzy of a start-up to hit a target. But there's something wrong with a start-up that can't learn.

This quick sketch of stagnant and chaotic strategies and the kind of clarity they both lack shows why clear strategies are rare. It's because they're hard to specify. They need to set aggressive goals to avoid stagnation. And they need to propose a way of achieving them that experience can help refine over time. Clear strategies are hard because they really force you to find out, if not to know, what you're talking about.

How Setting Testable Strategies Helps Alcoa and GE Learn from Experience

However rare, clear and testable strategies appear to be a requirement for firms to learn from experience. For example, both Alcoa and GE manage themselves by laying out clear, changing performance goals and strategic assumptions that they regularly put to the test. This section draws links between this practice, Rand Corporation's assumption-based planning, and Rita McGrath's and Ian MacMillan's discovery-driven planning.

Before he became secretary of the U.S. Treasury, Paul O'Neill served as CEO of Alcoa from 1987 until 2000. Alcoa revenue grew on average 23 percent per year from $1.5 to $23 billion over the period.[19] The record is especially remarkable in light of the fact that inflation was low at that time, no major, discontinuous new uses of aluminum emerged, and the company nevertheless grew largely organically. More remarkable still, O'Neill compiled the record over a period that saw fairly sharp commodity market downturns in 1991, 1993, and 1998.[20] Alcoa has proven a deft giant in a sector whose risk management needs have become paralyzingly complex.

After seven years at Toyota and several as a consultant, John Marushin became director of an internal consulting group that helped operating units implement the Alcoa Business System (ABS). He gives an anecdote illustrating the high adaptability of Alcoa operations. It also illustrates how Alcoa's adaptability depends on an environment that lets managers speculate about what matters most and test their ideas.[21]

The difficulty of meeting surges in customer needs through new ingot production led a smelting unit to hold thirty thousand tons of aluminum ingots in inventory. But the cost of financing that inventory made the smelter's ingots uncompetitive. Marushin's ABS team started by focusing the unit on what was critical for customer needs: on-time production of varying numbers of ingots, in this case. Then it tried to rank possible obstacles. Finally, it laid out detailed cause-and-effect scenarios for overcoming the most likely obstacles in enough detail to test them. Those scenarios were testable strategies.

Speeding up the changeover time for casting equipment in the smelter's ingot pit from six hours to twenty minutes turned out to have a big impact on production schedules. It let the operation produce all five of its products every day rather than just one type each week. And that let the unit meet changing customer needs without much inventory. "The process improvement was changeover in the pit," explains Marushin. "The system improvement was . . . the cash cost of the business."[22] He might have added plant flexibility, happier customers, and less pressure for smelter consolidation.

You might wonder whether the firm tried to match the adaptability of ABS at the level of its management system by systematically articulating testable corporate and divisional strategies. That turns out to be a good description of how Alcoa worked.

When Paul O'Neill became CEO, for example, he drafted the strategic vision that Alcoa would be "the best aluminum company in the world." And it would achieve this by being "a growing worldwide company dedicated to excellence through quality."[23] Instead of a bromide, the statement put forward two ideas that experience might have proved wrong. It asserted that quality was a route to excellence, which might have come as a surprise to many in a basic metals sector beset by declining costs in a globalizing market. And it asserted that growth was necessary to be best in class, suggesting growth was a necessary ingredient of not just size but quality. Results might have proved this vision wrong, and yet growth made the firm more agile than its competitors and quality reduced cost by reducing defects and waste.

What applied to the apex of the company applied to its operating units: every Alcoa operating manager articulated a clear aspiration for what he or she ran, together with a sense of how to achieve it. An example from a mine manager was to become "the most customer-oriented, quality-focused mine in Australia."[24] Marushin's consulting team asked each internal client what would have to happen for the unit to grow and gain market share according to its marketing plan and aspirations.[25]

Coincidentally Paul O'Neill served on the Rand Corporation's board of directors and later as its chairman at the time it published Jim Dewar's 1993 paper on assumption-based planning (ABP) for the U.S. Army.[26] Those initials may look familiar. In fact, ABP and ABS are close cousins.

Jim Dewar and his coauthors at Rand developed ABP to deal with highly uncertain environments. While U.S. military planners in the Cold War were able to work around a single future scenario, they point out that "during very uncertain times, such as those of today . . . [plans] that assume the likelihood of one particular world run the risk of being seriously wrong."[27]

For uncertain environments, they propose a planning process that starts with the key assumptions needed to project an outcome. Subsequent steps are to identify vulnerabilities of the key assumptions, indicators of those vulnerabilities, actions to shape outcomes favorably, and actions to hedge against unfavorable outcomes.

The Rand authors focus on what they call important assumptions. They define an assumption as "an assertion about some characteristic of the future that underlies the current operations or plans of an organization."[28] An assumption is important if "its negation would lead to significant changes in . . . current operations."[29] In other words, the assumptions of interest here could be wrong, and being wrong matters to results.

The hardest assumptions to identify are those we make implicitly. A simple example of an implicit assumption is, "The enemy cannot possibly approach by that route."[30] An example of one of the actual assumptions the Rand writers identified for their project was, "The Army will continue to play a primary role in maintaining global stability across the operational continuum."[31] It's a good example because there was little doubt about its importance, but it may no longer be true.

Of course, nothing in ABP can guarantee that you will identify all of the most important assumptions you're making, especially the implicit ones. This has been a recurring objection to ABP, and there's still disagreement whether it needs an answer. As Dewar and his coauthors note, the best remedy is repeated application of the process.[32]

Rand's ABP and Alcoa's ABS share more than a common patron in Paul O'Neill and a casual family resemblance. Both start by laying out the guesses we have to make in forming an expectation of future results that could lead to the biggest errors. For Alcoa managers, these guesses are strategic assumptions. Managers at different levels of the company will focus on assumptions about different things. But the assumptions must all be precise enough for performance results to test them. Alcoa is an example of a firm that makes itself adaptable by laying out strategies clear enough to be testable.

Rita McGrath and Ian MacMillan draw an even clearer connection between learning from experience and testable assumptions in a variation on ABP that they describe in *The Entrepreneurial Mindset*.[33] Their starting point is the refrain of nearly every manager they met who was responsible for a new business initiative subject to the intricate budgets of a modern enterprise planning system: "The ink would barely be dry when unfolding experience revealed the numbers to be wrong."[34]

What comes after the refrain tells you all about the health of the company. If top management asks, "What will you change going forward?" it's probably fine. If top management asks, "How can I rely on your numbers?" the firm may be in trouble. "An organization in which [the latter] is happening," write the authors, "is an organization deprived of permission to learn."[35]

McGrath and MacMillan call their version of Paul O'Neill's and Rand's solution *discovery-driven planning* (DDP).[36] DDP starts with a reverse income statement that forces you to work backward from an income target to the main assumptions at the level of income statement line items that you must make to arrive at it. Although I'll criticize the adequacy of reverse income statements for generating testable assumptions in the next chapter, they at least force you to make assumptions more specific than your final goal. The method's next step generates a more detailed list of assumptions about the project. Its last step defines milestones at which you should test the assumptions.

Two features of DDP stand out. Although it pushes you to proceed with a project without waiting for perfect information to fall into your lap, it never mistakes the assumptions that let you proceed for facts. And it focuses your energy on testing those assumptions, starting with the ones that could have the biggest impact on your target.

McGrath and MacMillan suggest that a form of assumption-led planning resembling DDP made it possible for the National

Aeronautics and Space Administration (NASA) to simplify and streamline the enormously complex problem of getting to the moon. "Through three programs," they write, "the manned Mercury program, Project Gemini, and, finally, the Apollo missions, which eventually led to the successful lunar landing, NASA's rocket scientists faced a massive, ongoing learning challenge."[37] The key was to specify for the milestones of each program "what its staff would have to learn to acquire maximum confidence to go on to the next stage."[38]

NASA's milestones represented major assumptions about what it would have to achieve to land someone on the moon. The most prominent ones were developing reliable launch and recovery technology and orbiting the earth. And the focus of each stage of the programs was to minimize uncertainty around the remaining unsettled assumptions that had the largest impact on program goals. "The organization specified, in other words, what assumptions needed to be tested and validated at each stage so that NASA staff would have the knowledge needed to go to the next stage."[39]

The methods and examples of *Entrepreneurial Mindset* show how managers can adapt more quickly to experience by laying out testable assumptions and goals. The biggest challenge tends to be making sure that those assumptions are specific enough to test— and not just broad requirements for the possibility of hitting goals. But there are a few firms that test their assumptions rigorously. GE appears to be one.

There are too many great resources on GE's Six Sigma version of continuous process improvement to review it in detail here.[40] Nevertheless, one aspect of it is central to this chapter's overview of how and why organizations need testable strategies to learn from experience. GE uses expectations about outcomes to guide every performance improvement effort. The firm is a monument to the idea that what you learn depends on what you expect.

It derives those expectations in part from customer requirements. I wish I could also report that GE has found a way to test the customer perspective on which it relies in setting goals such as quality targets. Since GE's growth no doubt broadens that perspective, I once thought its aggressive acquisition programs were a deliberate learning strategy. The firm won't generally justify a bid by what it expects to learn from the customers it's acquiring, however. GE may grow to learn, but it won't pay to learn.

The name "Six Sigma" reveals the most powerful way GE sets performance expectations across the myriad processes its businesses manage. It refers to the low probability of any result that is as far as six standard deviations above or below normal.[41] GE uses it as a goal for the rarity of defects in any measure of quality established to be critical to customer satisfaction. For example, an uptick in the frequency of defects in power turbine blades at a GE plant might push a quality measure from six to four sigma. The frequency of a defective result just four standard deviations above or below normal is a lot higher than that of a result six standard deviations away from normal.

One advantage of the goal is its utter lack of ambiguity. No matter what aspect of quality or what kind of process you're considering, it makes sense to measure the frequency of defects in the output of the process. The larger advantage, however, is that the measure is comparable across widely differing processes. Better still, the existence of a common quality standard or goal ensures a coordinated approach to quality in the ultimate product.

To take a simplistic example, suppose GE measured some aspect of the quality of raw material for its power turbine blades, as well as some aspect of quality of the finished product. It would make little sense to hold the material to a six sigma standard while holding the final product to a lower three sigma standard. Comparability in the levels of quality attained by the various parts of a production process makes sure no effort is wasted on quality at one stage only to be undermined by a quality breakdown at another.

The existence of a common quality standard promotes learning at GE because it sets an explicit expectation across complex production and service processes. Moreover, GE can raise or lower that expectation as it learns about any particular new product or service. If GE set its quality expectations for an entirely new product—let's say fuel cells—as high as its expectations for power turbines, process improvement for the new product would quickly bog down under an avalanche of missed goals. A new fuel cell division could aim instead at a relatively low quality bar such as three sigma, and then raise all aspects of its production processes gradually to the level of older products.

In one sense, it's obvious that the expectations embedded in a six sigma quality standard promote learning. When quality defects in a process rise above the expected level, the process owner must launch an effort to control them, and that effort requires learning about the root causes of the defects.

There's also a deeper sense in which GE's quality expectations drive continuous learning. The highest expectations are a very sensitive indication of how well the firm understands a business process. You need to know a lot about a process to think you can hold defects below one in a million. If your theory about ensuring quality is rich enough, you'll be in a good position to probe for weak assumptions when you miss a quality goal. It's a little bit like throwing darts at a dartboard. If the target has no sections marked off except the center, it's hard to make corrections. On a board with a lot of well-marked sections, however, you can make precise adjustments.

A stringent and consistent quality standard forces you to separate what you know about a process into a lot of well-marked compartments. And that lets you keep track of which precise changes in the process improve the quality of its outcomes. By forcing clarity in your expectations about what affects quality, the standard accelerates learning.

There's just one fly in the ointment. How do you define a defect? How do you tell which aspects of quality matter and what level of quality is acceptable for each? Like Motorola before it, GE starts with the voice of the customer. Through satisfaction surveys, after-sales calls, service interactions, and even interactive Web sites, quality teams determine customers' critical-to-quality

(CTQ) requirements. For example, on-time delivery might be a CTQ requirement. If so, GE finds out in what time interval delivery would be acceptable. Deliveries outside that interval are defects.

Enlisting customers in goal setting has a long and successful history going back to the earliest days of quality control. Customer-defined quality goals lead process owners to formulate expectations about how to meet them that experience can quickly test. Even so, there's always a chance that the customer may not be right. If you're serving a cadre of loyal customers who don't care about your product's color, for example, you're unlikely to brighten it even if the unserved larger market might care a lot about it.

Clay Christensen has explored the idea that the customer is not always right in *The Innovator's Dilemma*.[42] There he provides the memorable example of makers of cable-actuated construction equipment missing the needs of an emerging class of owners of tract homes after World War II. They needed agile backhoes and steam shovels that only the inferior technology of hydraulics, then in its infancy, could provide. Of course, hydraulics manufacturers came to dominate construction equipment. Customers of the cable-actuated equipment manufacturers weren't right for their future.

Before Christensen published his book in 1997, however, and even before GE adopted Six Sigma in 1997, I thought the firm had an answer to the dilemma posed by the customer who is not always right. I thought the answer was to buy more customers.

As a young Lehman Brothers banker in the early 1990s, I helped AT&T Capital build up its book of equipment leases and other forms of equipment finance by acquiring smaller finance companies. The other big buyer in every deal—often victorious—was GE Capital. GE Capital's due diligence team would often be heading out the door of a finance company that had put itself up for bid as the AT&T Capital team came in, or vice versa. When I asked GE Capital staff why they were so aggressive in acquiring finance companies, they would say, "We're buying customers."

In retrospect, what they meant was simply that they were buying business opportunities they could develop through careful management. The four current and former GE executives with whom I talked while writing this book insisted they wouldn't let a learning opportunity become an excuse for an aggressive bid. They all agreed that GE benefits from growth that broadens its customer perspective. But hard-to-measure considerations like learning can erode the discipline of an acquisition program. Perhaps this book can change that by providing more concrete ways to measure learning.

Happily, there are easier ways to draw up a testable strategy than embarking on an aggressive acquisition program. Chapter Two proposes a method for distilling the strategy relevant to a manager at any level of a firm to a short list of testable assumptions. Setting out a testable strategy is the first step in the guess-test system of performance management. Starting with guesses in the form of testable strategies, it lets you pick out facts that can improve decisions from large amounts of conflicting performance data and uses performance results to sharpen those strategies continuously.

2

GOALS, ASSUMPTIONS, AND THE EIGHT-LINE STRATEGY

> Both loud and silent single shots can cause a death;
> but not the same death.
>
> —*Donald Davidson*

This chapter shows how to construct the kind of testable performance strategies that are necessary, I believe, to learn from experience in today's information-overloaded organizations. The first section gives an overview of a method called *eight-line strategies* for distilling the strategy relevant to a manager at any level of a firm to a short list of critical assumptions. These assumptions lay the foundation for vastly simplified management reporting and performance reviews.

The next four sections flesh out the method with several rules of thumb:

- *Devise short-term milestones*—to make sure even long-term goals are testable in the short run.
- *Set 50-50 goals*—to extract as many lessons from experience as possible.
- *Lay out high-surprise assumptions*—to focus on factors that are both uncertain and high in impact.
- *Identify major risks and spillover effects*—to test assumptions about uncontrollable factors and undesired outcomes.

The section following the four rules provides a concrete example of an eight-line strategy. And the final section identifies the chapter's theme of testable strategies as a first step in the guess-test system of performance management. Starting with guesses in the form of testable strategies, this system helps you pick out facts that can improve decisions from piles of conflicting performance data. It uses performance results as a means of sharpening strategy continuously and not just a way to ensure execution.

A number of writers have contended that managers should focus on execution because strategy depends on it. But the last section argues that we can no more reduce strategy to execution than we can reduce goals to facts. An organization's prospects depend on the fitness of its strategy regardless of execution just as a species' future depends on the fitness of its DNA regardless of the health of individual members.

Eight-Line Paths

To learn anything from the heap of data our management information systems grind out, we need a basis for telling which metrics matter. The examples of Chapter One suggest that strategic assumptions—basically, our biggest bets or guesses—provide such a basis. The idea is to focus on the performance metrics that best test those assumptions and to try out new assumptions in place of the ones that fail.

This section proposes a method called eight-line strategies for distilling the strategy relevant to a manager at any level of a firm to a short list of critical assumptions. These assumptions lay the foundation for vastly simplified management reporting and performance reviews. The method reflects common themes from the planning and performance systems of the most adaptable McKinsey clients, Rand sponsors, BCG clients, Corporate Executive Board members, and national banks I've served since 1980. Three things distinguish these organizations: they make bold assumptions about the unknown as a matter of course, they spend their time looking for errors rather than trying to prove themselves right, and when they find an error in an assumption, they're quick to revise it and change course. Highly adaptable organizations are rare but diverse. What seems to bind them together is their use of some variation on the method I propose here.

Eight-line strategies are startlingly simple—you won't need to call a consultant or fire up your computer. Just draw eight horizontal lines on a piece of paper to serve as blanks for a list of assumptions (see Exhibit 2.1). Draw a column of shorter lines to the right for goals corresponding to them. Start filling in the template from the bottom with your final goal for the next month or quarter (depending on how often you review performance). For business leaders, this will often be a financial goal such as earnings, cash flow, or economic value added.[1] For operating executives, this could be a production or service target. For functional executives, it might be a procurement savings target, a sales goal, a goal for revenue from innovations, a targeted number of audit engagements, or a quality goal. The goal states what it is you believe you can deliver and by when if it's not obvious. The assumption specifies how you think you can deliver it given the contributing assumptions and goals in the lines above.

Exhibit 2.1 Eight-Line Strategies

Assumptions	Goals
_____	_____
_____	_____
_____	_____
_____	_____
_____	_____
_____	_____
_____	_____
_____	_____

The lines above the bottom are for the critical assumptions—the biggest bets or guesses—you must make in calculating your final goal. If the bottom line were a revenue goal, for example, the two lines above it might target units sold and price per unit—but only if your assumptions about how to achieve those targets are explicit. Describe the assumptions you must make that contribute to your final goal on the left and write down the values you expect to see for the quantities those assumptions describe on the right. To arrive at a production goal for a hand tool of 1,000 units, for example, you may find yourself making the assumptions that your fabrication team will complete 1,050 units with a 5 percent defect rate using current manufacturing processes.

Now erase each assumption that is a relatively sure bet, as well as its corresponding goal. The reason is that the purpose of this list is to identify what—as far as you can imagine—may go wrong. After erasing the settled assumptions corresponding to those sure bets, you should have a few spaces unfilled at the top.

The last step is to fill in the most important of what I'll call your implicit assumptions. Identifying implicit assumptions is one of the hardest things we do as managers, and it's probably the hardest part of any assumption-based approach to planning. The eight-line strategy framework nevertheless provides some clarity by dividing critical implicit assumptions into major risks and spillover effects. Some ideas for identifying these risks and side effects follow the sections on devising short-term milestones, setting 50-50 goals, and laying out high-surprise assumptions.

Rule 1: Devise Short-Term Milestones

This rule basically says that farsightedness is no excuse for ignoring the obstacles in front of you. It doesn't deny the value of a long-term perspective or imply that long-term vision and sustainability are unimportant. But without short-term indicators of progress, there can be no near-term learning. And without near-term learning, you cannot know whether you are making progress toward a long-term vision or a sustainable future.

Relating short-term indicators to long-term goals can be difficult, however. For example, think of a plan to break into a new market with a complex product requiring significant service. You may have projected the new market's potential based on its size and on your share of your existing markets. But if the new market is in a country you've never served before, you may have no idea how long it will take potential customers to trust you. What can you realistically promise in year one? What can you promise in year two?

The problem is that the sales process in your new market may take longer than a year. In such a case, you might have a terrific year and yet show no sales. So first-year sales by itself could be a terrible measure of progress. But if you set yourself a goal for sales over, say, a three-year period, you will have no way to tell whether you're on track until it's probably too late for corrective action. What would be a testable strategy?

The temptation in cases like this is to resort to the infamous hockey-stick plan. Just draw a line showing negligible sales or other deliverables for the first two or three years of the project and then a miraculous rise to the ultimate goal in its last year! To be fair, there are situations where worthwhile goals take many years to bear fruit. But hockey-stick plans insulate a project from review for however many years the handle of the hockey stick extends. How are we supposed to know what midterm course changes to make without some kind of review? Even with the best will in the world, a project leader has no basis for learning without a near-term challenge.

New business developers and research and development managers increasingly combat the temptation of distant goals with "fast-to-fail" methods. Faced with a choice of several possible new business opportunities, a fast-to-fail practitioner will first explore those allowing the earliest tests of success or failure. Since it's easier to find early signs that a venture destined to fail won't succeed than early proofs that an initiative destined to work out will definitely do so, the method focuses first on those projects with the earliest potential signs of failure. After all, if these projects fail, they will at least release resources sooner than the others would. And you learn a lot from mistakes.

As an example of a fast-to-fail method, Microsoft built two levels of short-term progress indicators into its development efforts for Office 2000. In the firm's "milestone process," developers split the functionality they were trying to create into development stages marked off by milestones with fixed dates. But instead of letting a milestone's date slip until they had delivered all of its functionality, developers made whatever compromises on functionality were necessary to protect the date. The effect was to pull forward the times at which major parts of the system were available for testing.

Microsoft also used "daily builds" to allow daily testing of the emerging system. Under the discipline of this process, programmers submitted code at the end of each day for overnight testing. Work did not resume until the team could fix most of the bugs emerging from the previous increment of programming. This way, the team constantly tested its assumptions about solving the larger development challenges of the project. Daily builds not only pinpoint what causes problems but help teams learn as they go.[2]

Microsoft's milestone process and daily builds are part of a software development movement called extreme programming (XP). Frequent testing is at the heart of XP, and at the heart of its testing practices are unit tests. These are lines of code that put part of a program through its paces. They must be small and fast because programmers will eventually build a whole suite of unit tests checking each thing a program does.

Before integrating new code into a program, the development team runs the program with the new code through all of its unit tests on a separate computer and debugs it until it passes them. This discipline has given rise to a practice called "test-first" programming, in which a programmer designs a new unit test before writing the code it is supposed to check.[3]

The test-first ethic of extreme programming shows a practical way to devise short-term indicators for even the most challenging long-term goals. It suggests starting with what you would have to observe if things were going well. For example, you might expect a large percentage of the prospects in a new market to have agreed to see you again at a fixed date in the future if things were on track. An alternative might be to ask your prospects in an initial visit how much time they expect they would need for a decision if in fact the product were perfect for them. You could then revisit them at a later date and compare their new estimate of time to decision with what they originally told you.

The comparison might be biased in some cases, but it could also give an indication of progress toward goals that are otherwise directly measurable only in the distant future. The test-first lesson for business leaders is to articulate what you would expect to observe soon if you were really on track toward your ultimate goal and then test that expectation.

In sum, the reason for short-term goals in an eight-line strategy is not to reinforce short-term thinking. It is to force early learning about ultimate goals, whatever they may be. Those early tests become the practical focus of an eight-line strategy not because long-term visions are unimportant to impatient shareholders but because there is little that our near-term experience can directly tell us about whether we understand them.

Rule 2: Set 50-50 Goals

Nobody likes to miss a goal, but it's hard to think of any example of learning from experience that does not involve some kind of surprise or mistaken expectation—in short, some form of missed goal. A missed goal forces you to change your strategy or change the goal. More than a necessary evil, missed goals may be vital for learning.

This seems to hold even in everyday examples of learning like making a wrong turn in search of a shortcut. It's true that you may not have formulated an explicit goal (much less an eight-line strategy). Nevertheless, you could have done so: you could have said your goal was to reduce the drive home by taking a new route—and you missed it.

So although nobody likes to fall short of their goals, it appears that missing them is critical for learning. If that's the case, it's a mistake to set expectations so low we rarely fail to meet them.

Information theory suggests we will generally learn the most from goals set at a level we have an equal likelihood of making or missing.[4] Designed to measure the information content of messages and the capacity of communications channels, information theory focuses on how much you learn from typical runs of an uncertain experiment such as throwing dice. The conclusion makes intuitive sense too. If you have an equal chance of making or missing a goal, the goal represents what you actually expect. So variances from it will show whether your expectation was realistic.

The problem is that goals you have only a 50 percent chance of hitting can be discouraging. Imagine how you would feel if you knew you would earn a bonus in only two of the next four years! But all this really means is that goals that test assumptions and goals that motivate people serve two distinct functions. There's no reason to set the two kinds of goals at the same level.

Companies are increasingly using multilevel goals to motivate and measure performance. The Corporate Executive Board, for example, has set "worthy" and "adequate" goals for many of its key performance indicators. Practice still varies widely, but organizations are starting to set a high goal for planning purposes at a level they expect to hit half of the time and a lower goal for purposes of determining incentive compensation that they expect to hit more often, between 65 percent and 90 percent of the time. A goal set at the 90 percent level, for example, will be considerably lower than the corresponding 50 percent goal, and nine out of ten units, teams, or individuals can expect to hit it.

Rule 3: Lay Out High-Surprise Assumptions

Once you've devised a short-term measure of long-term success and set a goal reflecting what you really think you can deliver, it's time to list your key assumptions about how to deliver it. You may feel you need to make more than four or five critical assumptions to hit the final goal in an eight-line strategy. The method nevertheless asks you to prioritize them. The challenge is telling which ones are not just important but able to explain large potential performance surprises. I call these *high-surprise assumptions*.

There are innumerable possible criteria for prioritizing assumptions. Fortunately, our purpose in selecting assumptions for an eight-line strategy is quite specific: to create a tool for simplifying management decisions and making organizations more adaptable. These are the very interests in play when managers select vital risks for close monitoring and mitigation, since risk managers seek simple rules and flexible responses.

For our purposes, then, the risk manager's criteria for what matters should be a useful guide to which of our assumptions matter. The most widespread way to rank risks is by worst-case potential impact.[5] Worst-case impact focuses on two things: the variability of a risk factor and the sensitivity of some set of results to it. Variability and sensitivity apply directly to the challenge of identifying high-surprise assumptions.

Variability distinguishes settled from unsettled assumptions. Settled assumptions are those in little danger of being wrong. For example, it may be critically important to an assumption about your production schedule that all three of your factory foremen show up to work each day. But they nearly always do. The assumption may be important, but it's not likely to be wrong. Settled assumptions should not take up scarce space in an eight-line strategy.

This is the principal flaw in McGrath's and MacMillan's method of reverse income statements mentioned in Chapter One.[6] You're only a little likelier to hit a profit goal than to meet the kind of assumptions you derive by projecting the line items of an income statement that would yield it. But assumptions about how to achieve a goal should be much more unlikely—or much more specific—than the goal. Otherwise those assumptions amount to saying you'll hit the goal any way you can. And in that case, experience will tell you little about how best to achieve it.

For an oversimplified example, imagine your goal is to earn $10,000 of profit, and you assume you can do so by selling $100,000 of business books at a cost of $90,000. It's true that the revenue and cost assumptions are a little more specific than the profit assumptions—other combinations of revenue and cost yield $10,000 of profit. But those assumptions are still quite vague. The revenue assumption, for example, is consistent with a wide range of combinations of book prices and numbers of volumes.

Nothing in the method of reverse income statements forces you to stop with broad assumptions about revenue and cost, of course. But the point is that the method demands nothing more than assumptions about the decomposition of a financial goal. To learn how to achieve a financial goal, however, requires going further. One must hazard a guess about an action plan that will realize it and then test that plan. You know your assumptions are specific enough that you can learn from them if there's a good chance you'll hit your goal and yet fail to do so in the way you assumed you would.

Sensitivity distinguishes assumptions that have a big impact on projected results from those whose impact is small. The amount of time it takes your sales prospects to return a call may be highly uncertain, for example. But if you are scheduling sales visits long in advance, it may not matter. If your projected results are not sensitive to an assumption, that assumption probably does not require the focus of an eight-line strategy.

Here, then, is a framework for prioritizing assumptions. List the ones you think are most important. Separate those that are highly unsettled from the ones that are more settled. And of those that are highly unsettled, focus on the ones to which your projected results are most sensitive.

For example, suppose you are head of procurement and have committed to cut 1 percent from your company's costs. Let's say you have assumed that (1) your team will suffer little attrition in the coming year, (2) it will maintain the savings it has secured in past years, and (3) you will be able to achieve significant new savings in the professional services arrangements of the firm's finance and legal departments. If previously secured savings have persisted in the past, then your second assumption is fairly settled, and you would not need to include it in an eight-line strategy for procurement. And if attrition has not had a material effect on procurement results in past years, you can also exclude your first assumption since results do not depend heavily on it. That would leave your final assumption about savings from the procurement of finance and legal professional services as a high-surprise assumption that belongs in an eight-line strategy.

This process of triage will probably leave you with three to five critical strategic assumptions. Write them in the spaces of your eight-line strategy above your assumption for a final goal. These assumptions—the unsettled ones to which your results are most sensitive—are precisely the ones most likely to account for the biggest misses.

The focus of eight-line strategies on unsettled assumptions makes them different from Kaplan and Norton's balanced scorecards and most other scorecard planning methods. By enumerating all of an organization's major cause-and-effect relationships, balanced scorecards incorporate more and more settled assumptions over time. Settled assumptions may serve a surveillance or motivational purpose, but as the next chapter will argue, they are not central to the challenge of learning from experience.

Including settled assumptions in a short list of key indicators produces some strange results. In their book *Strategy Maps*, for example, Kaplan and Norton urge managers to devise a metric and goal for their organization's "strategic job families." They argue that strategic human resources planning must focus on the vital few jobs having the greatest impact. As an example, they cite John Bronson, vice president of human resources at Williams-Sonoma, who "estimated that people in only five job families determine 80 percent of his company's strategic priorities."[7]

This emphasis on strategic job families is uncomfortable because it seems to create a permanent strategic underclass in an organization's workforce. Of course, Kaplan and Norton are just trying to restrict the focus of balanced scorecards, which always risk growing too large. But those scorecards purport to cover every factor that's really important, so if the training for your job family is off the scorecard, you're out of luck.

This is a shame because it's unclear what practical purpose is served by trying to include every high-impact factor, regardless of whether it's variable, on a scorecard. Reserving scorecards for unsettled assumptions—and, in the case of human capital measures, for a strategy's current new job requirements—would provide the focus Kaplan and Norton seek without creating the implication of a permanent strategic underclass.

It's a little mysterious why there are rarely more than a few unsettled working assumptions on which our results strongly depend. Vilfredo Pareto concluded from his classic work on probability distributions that only a vital few factors drive most results.[8] And quality control methods such as Six Sigma often start by identifying the "vital few" root causes of a quality threat. But why the vital are few is still mysterious.

It may be simply that the kinds of assumptions we make, risks we track, and root causes we identify all resemble scores in a game of craps. The sixes, sevens, and eights we so often see when we roll two dice are common because they reflect so many underlying combinations of the individual dice. However precisely we may think we have expressed our assumptions, they too reflect averages of the results of processes too fine to observe. No doubt the effects of those microprocesses often cancel each other out just as a low roll of "one" and a high roll of "six" still yield the craps average of "seven." If this is the case, it makes sense to focus on the handful of high-surprise assumptions characterizing rare combinations of underlying processes that, like snake eyes and double sixes, stand out from the norm.

Rule 4: Identify Major Risks and Spillover Effects

By now you will probably have filled five lines of an eight-line strategy, and you will have been able to do so using just what you know about the results you project. But what can you say about what you don't know? We make implicit assumptions about what we don't know, and they too have a place in an eight-line strategy. They should appear as prudent confessions of ignorance. Sometimes it's even worth saying explicitly, "No other assumption could have a big impact on my results *as far as I know*."

Identifying implicit assumptions will always be hard. Think how many business breakthroughs have really amounted to the identification of implicit assumptions others had missed. Microsoft exposed the error in assuming that hardware controlled the technology market. Toyota exposed the error in assuming the length of production runs must drive manufacturing efficiency. Merrill Lynch wrap accounts showed what was wrong with the assumption that savers will trust only insured banks for their transaction accounts. Southwest Airlines exposed the mistaken assumption that hub-and-spoke networks will always outperform point-to-point ones, and Duke Energy and Southern Company showed that power generation and delivery did not have to be integrated.

It helps to recognize two main categories of implicit assumptions. One is tacit assumptions about risks, and the other is tacit assumptions about the side effects of our strategies.[9] Implicit assumptions about risks could include, for example, the caveat that the other assumptions of a strategy presume relatively stable energy prices or exchange rates. Implicit assumptions about side effects often stipulate that the negative consequences of a strategy are negligible compared to its principal benefit. An example might be the assumption that a firm's activities will not cause much pollution.

Scenario planning may help you try to envision the worst unrevealed risks and side effects that threaten your strategies, and dozens of books promise to reduce the identification of risks and unexpected side effects to simple methods. But there can be no fail-safe method. Most implicit assumptions are implicit because you need experience to reveal them.

The good news is that it can be very helpful to separate the challenge of identifying your most fateful implicit assumptions into the two tasks of envisioning risks and anticipating side effects. They seem to respond to different skills—operating knowledge helps identify risks, while a general knowledge of customer markets and business environments helps anticipate side effects—and different colleagues may help you think through them. But the best discipline of all may be to force yourself to identify one of each kind of implicit assumption every time you revise an eight-line strategy.

The following taxonomy of uncertainties may help you think of implicit assumptions about risks and side effects. Uncertainties affecting production processes include operating risks, supply chain risks, technology performance risks, risks to your workforce, and risks to your assets. Uncertainties affecting customers, markets, and operating environments include security and political risks, risks in customer behavior, competitive risks, regulatory risks, and financial market and economic risks.[10]

It's probably too much to hope you can identify the most severe outstanding risk or side effect threatening your plans when you first write down an eight-line strategy. The one consolation is that you will get better with experience. The advantage of eight-line strategies lies in what you learn by systematically revising them every time you review interim results. Risks that don't materialize, for example, should eventually give way in an eight-line strategy to others. Anticipated side effects that prove serious, on the other hand, should evolve into explicit assumptions.

There seem to be no major categories of implicit assumptions other than risks and side effects. Anything a strategy assumes that is not about its effects must be about what causes them. So the question is whether there can be an implicit assumption about the effects of a strategy that is not about its side effects or an implicit assumption about the uncontrollable drivers of a strategy that is not about its risks.

It's hard to imagine what an implicit assumption about the effects of a strategy could address if not its side effects. But the question as to whether there are implicit assumptions about the uncontrollable drivers of a strategy that are not about its risks is tougher. Since we have already listed the assumptions about how to achieve a goal on which we think our results most heavily depend, however, the only critical assumptions we're missing—assuming we're right—address the factors we don't control. In other words, our explicit assumptions about how to produce a projected result should cover everything except the risks that threaten those assumptions.

If this is right, then once you write down the biggest risks and most serious side effects of your strategy, you are done. Exhibit 2.2 provides a template for identifying the assumptions of an eight-line strategy. If you have a free space you may want to reserve it for a final generic assumption: the assumption that nothing else is as important as the other assumptions on the list. In some performance systems, it will make sense to set a confidence interval around your final projected result in the space reserved for the generic assumption's goal. This will let you test your level of confidence in the other assumptions when you measure actual performance. But for most, this is unnecessary.

Example of an Eight-Line Strategy

Let's say you run a clothing boutique, and your landlord offers you a small connected space for $8,000 per month. It's within sight of the storefront window, and you think you could hang kimono in it. You feel you need $12,000 of monthly gross profit to justify the hassle of a new line and write this down as your goal. Say you

Exhibit 2.2 Identifying the Assumptions of an Eight-Line Strategy

What's your best single
measure of success?

1. _____

What are the main factors determining actual results?	Which of these have the biggest impact on results?	Which are the most uncertain?
_____	_____	2. _____
_____	_____	3. _____
_____	_____	4. _____
_____	_____	5. _____
_____	_____	
_____	_____	
_____		
_____		

	What are the biggest risks or uncontrollable factors?	Which are the least predictable?
	_____	6. _____
	_____	7. _____
	_____	
	_____	

What's the biggest
potential harmful
side effect?

8. _____

assume that your current daily rate of 150 customers stays steady; 5 percent of the customers now visiting the store would buy a kimono if they could; the kimono will draw 10 percent more customers than you would otherwise see; 50 percent of these will be prepared to buy given your excellent taste; and you expect a $40 profit per kimono. You think the two biggest risks are whether there will be 20 days per month of weather conducive to shopping

Exhibit 2.3 Eight-Line Strategy for New Kimono Line

Assumptions	Goals
Steady daily customer rate	150
Will buy kimono if available	5 percent
Rate increase due to kimono	10 percent
Kimono seekers ready to buy	50 percent
Profit per kimono	$40
Likely shopping days per month	20
Cannibalization	None
New monthly revenue	$12,000

and whether the kimono will cannibalize your existing lines. A summary might look like Exhibit 2.3.

This simple exercise may seem hardly worth the effort. Yet as we'll see in the next chapter, it provides a short, crisp list of numbers worth tracking. You may change your mind about which numbers to track at the end of the month, but you will have learned something important about the business if you do. Suppose, for example, that the assumptions about existing customers hold up, but fewer than half of the new customers who come into your store for the kimono buy one. Your eight-line strategy in later months would probably concentrate on assumptions about what drives sales to these new customers.

Why Testable Strategies Matter

This chapter and the previous one make the case that learning from experience requires strategic assumptions and goals clear enough to be testable. BP's failure to learn from repeated mistakes in its American operations is a cautionary example. These chapters also argue that strategies clear enough to test are extraordinarily rare. Most organizations pursue stagnant or chaotic strategies that prove hard to test in the short run.

Alcoa and GE use plans built around testable assumptions to adapt to change. That's no accident, according to Rand

Corporation's assumption-based planning and McGrath's and MacMillan's discovery-driven planning: adaptability requires testable assumptions. This chapter proposes eight-line strategies for distilling any unit's plans to a short list of critical assumptions. It pares back unnecessary parts of earlier assumption-based systems and adds a few details needed to make sure the assumptions it generates are testable and really say something. Rules of thumb focus on devising short-term milestones, setting 50-50 goals, laying out high-surprise assumptions, and identifying major risks and spillover effects. They lay the foundation for vastly simplified management reporting and performance reviews.

The aspiration is that testable strategies will provide the first step in a planning and performance approach that can improve decisions despite masses of conflicting performance data. This approach will use performance data to sharpen strategy continuously and not just to ensure execution. Eight-line strategies make a down payment on that promise by putting strategy at the heart of performance management.

This may seem eminently logical, but it's hardly uncontroversial. Consider that you're reducing strategy to a short list of assumptions and goals, and those assumptions are essentially guesses about how your business works. Many managers have a serious problem with the idea of guessing their way to better performance in the face of change.

Reflecting this queasiness, several writers claim that managers should focus on execution since strategy depends on it.[11] Strategy is fluffy; execution is real. I suppose you could reply that while great performance results naturally require great execution, strategy matters too. This book, however, makes no pretense of being balanced. The view on offer here is that strategy is central to managers' roles in two ways that execution is not. First, strategy is central to learning and adaptation, which managers must coordinate. And second, strategies hold firms together.

The next chapter shows that strategy is central to learning and adaptation because of its power to simplify decisions in the face of change and uncertainty. That power to simplify decisions becomes especially important as growing databases make our operating environments more complex. Strategy can throw a spotlight on what really matters in those complex environments. The manager may initially aim the spotlight at an exit or the actor's feet but over time will become more adept. To become more adept, we must organize ourselves to refine our strategies over time in the light of experience. That is the subject of the rest of the book.

You might still object that management boils down to execution because there can't be any real difference between two strategies that doesn't reflect a difference in execution.[12] In other words, strategy reduces to execution, and that's a good thing because execution is something you can measure. Besides, there are dozens of stories of brilliant strategies that failed because of boneheaded execution. If you get execution right, runs the argument, strategy is redundant.

This argument is very good news for consultants because you can charge more for an engagement on executing a strategy than for a strategy audit. But I think it's wrong. Strategy is like a blackboard on which we write what we learn in the course of execution. Pursuing perfect execution without a strategy is like pursuing chaotic strategies. How can you tell which aspects of execution are working if you don't compare your results with some expectation? And what is a strategy but an expectation? We can no more reduce strategy to execution than we can reduce goals to facts.

The American philosopher Donald Davidson shows you couldn't do without abstractions like expectations, goals, and thoughts even if you could map them all to something as physical as brain states. We would still need those expectations, goals, and thoughts to pick out the brain states that matter. He considers the objection—which you might imagine coming from a consultant specializing in execution—that just because a loud shot kills something doesn't mean its loudness made a difference.[13]

Davidson doubts this marginalizes abstractions like loudness, goals, or expectations. He acknowledges that a silent shot might similarly cause a death, but it could not be the same death because it could not be the same shot. Loudness can pick out a shot that matters even if we don't think loudness matters. It's a powerful argument because it reminds us that a strategy can pick out the aspects of execution that matter even if we doubt great strategies can make a difference without competent execution.

In addition to their central role in learning and adaptation, strategies hold firms together. BP's recent troubles show that an organization's divisions may stop benefiting from one another's experience if they develop their strategies independently. Yet this chapter suggests something stronger: the relevance of one business unit's experience to the strategic planning of another determines whether they belong in the same firm.

That won't be news to GE, whose Global Leadership Meetings bring the company's top six hundred executives together every January to share best practices. If those practices are mutually relevant and yet hard for managers to discover without the help of GE's operating system and management meetings, then GE's corporate structure truly enhances the value of its various operating units.

But it will be news to the hundreds of corporate centers that delegate planning to close-to-the-customer operating units and think they can then ensure their relevance by offering those units low-cost shared services. Shared services include functions like cash accounting, facilities management, and benefits. The transaction costs they incur are real—in fact, just the kind that Coase thought companies could sometimes manage more efficiently than markets. But third-party providers like Bangalore-based Infosys Technologies now offer many of these services at low cost to the smallest firms. Transaction cost management cannot justify expensive corporate centers as it did before information technologies empowered efficient third-party processors. The company that can offer its business units nothing but shared services should probably break up.

Few multidivisional companies are breaking up under the pressure of cheap third-party service providers, however. It may be that CEOs can hold disparate business units together through sheer force of will. But it's more likely that the corporate structure of many large companies provides information benefits like GE's. The relevance of operating units' results to sister units' plans or strategies could be the glue that holds these firms together even as they outsource functions like mad. Strategic relevance could be the friction in the system that explains which corporations hold together today the way transaction costs explained the scope of companies in Coase's time.

You might agree that strategy is central to managers' roles in ways that execution is not—that it is central to learning and adaptation and holds firms together—and still have some qualms about this book's focus on strategy. You could still say it asks you to guess your way to better performance in the face of change or uncertainty. Why should that have any hope of working?

A partial answer is that we don't improve performance just by guessing about strategy but by what we do with those guesses after we test them. A full answer has to wait for the next few chapters, but even this partial one has some compelling cousins. Karl Popper argued that science owes its achievements not to any method for generating great theoretical conjectures but to its discipline in testing and revising them.[14] He wrote:

> I see our scientific theories as human inventions—nets designed by us to catch the world. . . . What we aim at is truth: we test our theories in the hope of eliminating those which are not true. In this way we may succeed in improving our theories—even as instruments: in making nets which are better and better adapted to catch our fish, the real world. Yet they will never be perfect instruments for this purpose. They are rational nets of our own making, and should not be mistaken for a complete representation of the real world in all its aspects; not even if they are highly successful; not even if they appear to yield excellent approximations to reality.[15]

In other words, the value of a scientific theory lies not in anyone's ability to tell that it's true but in our ability to put it to a test, find errors, and improve it.

It's no coincidence that Popper wrote about theories as "nets which are better and better adapted." He ultimately viewed science as an adaptive or evolutionary process. Evolutionary theory also puts guesses to work in the form of random genetic mutation. But it would be a mistake to think that you can ascribe the results of evolution to chance because evolution also involves natural selection. And natural selection is anything but random. As Richard Dawkins puts it, "Emphasizing that mutation *can* be random is our way of calling attention to the crucial fact that, by contrast, selection is sublimely and quintessentially *non*-random. It is ironic that this emphasis on the contrast between mutation and the non-randomness of selection has led people to think that the whole theory is a theory of chance."[16]

Like the randomness of genetic mutations, the arbitrariness of our strategic assumptions helps us search out possibilities. But there is nothing arbitrary or random about reviewing results to see which assumptions don't work.

The parallel between natural selection and testing strategic assumptions puts the very growth of our organizations into a new light. Business writers increasingly compare companies with biological species because companies compete to grow in exacting markets much as species compete to propagate in tough environments.[17] The comparison implies that strategy works like a firm's DNA. Think of it: your strategy undergoes potentially arbitrary change whenever you change your mind about your business, the change has an impact on how you compete, and success tends to reinforce the strategy.

This has the startling implication that in some ways, the fitness of a firm's strategy is more important than its results. After all, the future of a species depends on the fitness of its DNA regardless of the health of its individual members. You might even say that the health of the individuals shapes the fitness of the DNA.

By the same token, you might think of the interim results of a firm as a way to increase the fitness of its strategy, and the fitness of its strategy as the key to its future.

If this is right, growth has an importance apart from the opportunities and benefits it creates for an organization's clients, staff, and investors. Growth tests the organization's strategy. Firms that don't try to grow faster than their markets put themselves under less pressure to learn and adapt. Their strategies become stagnant, and they become less resilient.

This perspective sees growth not just as an end in itself but as a means to a further end. Instead of learning to grow, you might think of organizations growing to learn. Growth increases the fitness of an organization's strategy by forcing it to adapt—but only if it's testable. It's time to turn to the issue of testing.

3

KNOWING WHAT MATTERS

Balanced scorecards were born to free those who use them. Yet everywhere their users lie in chains.

Balanced scorecards are supposed to simplify the manager's problem of knowing which possible performance measures matter. Robert Kaplan and David Norton introduced balanced scorecards to the public in 1992 and published their first book on the management tool in 1996.[1] In addition to indicators measuring financial results, they recommend that organizations select indicators measuring performance from three other perspectives: customer satisfaction, the efficiency of internal processes, and learning and development. Since these last three perspectives give rise to leading indicators of performance, they balance the short-term orientation of a purely financial perspective's lagging indicators. The four perspectives also reflect broad causal relations from human capital development, to process improvement, to greater customer satisfaction, to financial success. Measuring indicators in all four perspectives therefore should provide a picture of whether an organization is doing what is necessary to achieve its objectives.

A survey in 2000 of 170 executives using balanced scorecards found that 47 percent were dissatisfied with them, however.[2] A Dutch survey in 1998 found 70 percent of executives were dissatisfied with them.[3] And a 2004 study of the results of forty-two Canadian firms over the three years following their implementation of balanced scorecards found no significant performance improvements in returns on sales or assets.[4]

Even more telling are the common complaints of executives who use balanced scorecards. Operating managers, financial executives, and department heads report that although there is always a need to add new indicators to a balanced scorecard, there is rarely agreement on which old ones to delete. As a result, metrics relentlessly accrete to balanced scorecards the way coral accretes to reefs.

There are two puzzles here. The first is how anything as seemingly innocuous as a balanced scorecard could cause dissatisfaction. The second is why, despite the authors' warnings to keep them simple, balanced scorecards nevertheless have become towering scrap heaps of used metrics.

The first puzzle should become clearer by the end of the next chapter, after the description of an alternative way to determine which performance measures matter. The key to the second puzzle may be that the pursuit of balance in performance reporting somehow leads to a paralyzing demand for more information that we can never fulfill. That makes the questionable role of balance in performance reporting a good introduction to the problem of knowing what matters. This and the next chapter argue that knowing what matters demands a planning and performance approach that derives performance metrics or indicators from key strategic assumptions—and not from balanced lists of outputs and the inputs they require, as most scorecard applications seem to do.

The best way to see why the pursuit of balance in performance reporting might lead to endless demands for data is through an analogy. News reporting turns out to be a rich one. The next section uses it to show that however important it may be to balance our short-term and long-term concerns, the pursuit of balance in what we measure reflects confusion about why we measure it.

The second section tries to clear up that confusion by defining *relevance*. It characterizes the kind of relevance we seek in performance metrics as relevance not to types of businesses or problems but to types of solutions. Specifically, it defines the relevance of a performance indicator with respect to assumptions about what will achieve a strategy's goals. A performance indicator is relevant to a strategic assumption, according to the definition, if the assumption's truth or falsity greatly affects the results expected. This definition will pick out the performance metrics most worth watching.

Whether they know it or not, most organizations use a starkly different definition of relevance. Their performance metrics ignore strategy altogether, track red herrings, or get lost in endless demands for more data. As a result, they tend to become less adaptable or mired in complexity. The last three sections of this chapter illustrate these fates with three companies in Kaplan's and Norton's Balanced Scorecard Collaborative, a group of businesses that share practices in the use of balanced scorecards for strategic planning and performance management.

Chapter Four turns from cautionary tales to positive prescriptions. It shows how adaptive companies learn from experience by deriving performance metrics from key assumptions. The idea of deriving performance indicators from key assumptions promises to simplify your planning and performance process dramatically. But to realize that promise, you need to identify which metrics are most relevant to your assumptions. The chapter introduces the metrics matrix, a tool to help you determine which indicators best test each of your key assumptions from an eight-line strategy— that is, which few measures you really want to watch. And it too requires only pen and paper.

Chapter Four concludes with a diagnosis of balanced scorecards suggesting that for all their advantages, they rarely test strategies. What they tend to test is something quite different: requirements for success. The problem is that we rarely mistake requirements but often pursue the wrong strategy. By testing something that is rarely wrong, balanced scorecards can lead to a false sense of infallibility.

A Quiet Day on the Tigris

The best way to see why pursuing balance in performance reporting might lead to endless demands for data is through an analogy. The analogy shows that however important it may be to balance our short-term and long-term concerns, the pursuit of balance in what we measure reflects confusion about why we measure it. So let's look at another kind of call for balance in reporting.

Partly on the basis of its campaign for "fair and balanced" news reporting, Rupert Murdoch's Fox Broadcasting Company grew from a start-up in 1986 to the top-ranked network among U.S. viewers between ages eighteen and forty-nine in 2005. Nor has the call for balance in news reporting stopped with Fox's efforts to increase its market share. It has become a common refrain in criticism of American news coverage.

How would you respond to a call for balance if you were editing newspaper stories about Iraq in the years following the 2003 U.S. invasion? Let's say conservative readers were upset because most of your reporters' stories were about violence and instability. You might be tempted to look for good news, but there's a risk: if you allowed so much as one happy story, about, say, the construction of a new school, to bump one story about a ghastly urban bombing, your credibility could suffer.

As an alternative, you might try to cover Iraq so extensively that you would never have to bump a discouraging story for an encouraging one. But where would your coverage stop? Would you publish a story about a teacher who took in a stray cat? If not, how would you decide which stories were important enough to publish and which ones were not? And what would you do if your criterion for importance yielded a lot more discouraging stories than encouraging ones? You would be back where you started.

At this point, you may well ask what purpose balanced news reporting serves. For example, is the point of balanced conflict reporting to help readers determine whether living conditions are improving or worsening? We've just seen that editors have to apply some criterion of importance in choosing stories. If that's the case, doesn't balanced reporting just help readers determine whether editors think conditions are improving?

There's something wrong here. There has to be a way for newspaper readers to extract a view of the world that's independent of the editor's view. The very fact that people draw diverging conclusions from newspaper stories shows that readers extract independent views all the time.

Reporting—balanced or otherwise—must serve some other purpose. So what's the alternative to helping readers draw conclusions about a situation as if they were starting with a blank slate? It must be helping readers draw conclusions about their own current views of the situation. In the case of Iraq, for example, the purpose of reporting might be to help readers check whether they're right about living conditions there.

This view of the purpose of reporting gives you, as an editor, a clear principle for choosing news stories: choose the stories that will challenge most readers' expectations. These are the stories, after all, that will best test their assumptions, and that seems to be a purpose that news reporting really can serve.

In the case of Iraq, on this view, you would select stories that challenge most readers' beliefs about conditions on the ground. If most readers expect peaceful reconstruction, you would serve them best with stories about violent setbacks challenging that expectation. If most readers expect uninterrupted violence, you would serve them best with stories about unexpected progress or a quiet day on the Tigris.

This view about what to pursue in reporting is counterintuitive. If the purpose of reporting is to help readers test their beliefs, then a story will naturally have different effects on readers with divergent views. However accurate and objective a news story may be, in other words, we may have to resign ourselves to debating what it means.

Of course, this is what we do all the time. All that debate makes a lot more sense if the point of reporting is to test our prior beliefs. Besides, we never really approach a news story without expectations. We always have some expectations about what we choose to read. It's probably unrealistic to think reporting helps readers draw conclusions as if they were starting with a blank slate.

This is where the analogy of balanced news reporting bears strongly on balanced performance reporting. Just as readers approach every news report with a set of expectations, managers approach every performance period with expectations about results. The argument in Chapters One and Two that managers should clarify their most important strategic assumptions applies directly to these expectations. If news reporting really serves to test readers' prior beliefs, the purpose that performance reporting can best serve may be to test the strategic assumptions behind each manager's expectations.

This view of the purpose of performance reporting is counter-intuitive too. It suggests that what you measure should depend on what you assume. You can see just how counterintuitive that is from the questions it raises about balanced scorecards.

The idea that what you measure depends on what you assume challenges the importance of balance in performance reporting—between long-term and short-term goals, for example. Your key strategic assumptions will not necessarily fall evenly across a balanced scorecard's financial, customer satisfaction, process efficiency, and learning and development perspectives. For example, there may be a lot more uncertainty around your internal process assumptions than your customer preference assumptions. Why, in that case, would you need balance between the customer satisfaction and process efficiency indicators you track?

Yet Kaplan and Norton had a very good reason to advocate balanced performance reporting. In their experience, too many executives focus on short-term financial goals and ignore the customer satisfaction, process efficiency, and capability development requirements of sustainable, long-term success. What could be wrong with measuring a balanced set of short-term and long-term success factors?

What's wrong is that once you start pursuing balance in your performance reports, there's no end to it. As most of us know from painful experience with long, confusing management reports, the solution to any question about scorecards tends to be more indicators. If you can think of an indicator that tests a critical, unsettled strategic assumption, measure it. And if you can think of customer, process, or capability indicators that balance your current area of strategic focus, measure them too. You may even persuade yourself it's your duty to track more indicators if you've spent a lot of money on an expensive enterprise planning system. And yet it's the relentless demand to track more indicators that forces us to buy bigger and better planning systems.

You may be tempted to say that once you've identified one performance goal from each of the three nonfinancial perspectives Kaplan and Norton identify—customer satisfaction, process efficiency, and learning and development—you're done. But it doesn't work that way. Suppose you identify an aspect of customer satisfaction to measure for the sake of some notion of balance in your picture of firm performance. The balance imperative will apply with the same force to your customer satisfaction picture. Soon you'll be tracking more indicators of what your customers think of you.

In sum, our management reports are becoming telephone books for reasons not so different from the call for balanced news reporting. The call for balanced news reporting, however, seems confused. It assumes we approach news stories without expectations, whereas what we really need from the news is some test of how our expectations are doing. As a result of the confusion, the Iraq editor who tries to address every call for balanced reporting may soon find himself editing stories about cats around Baghdad.

That looks a lot like the unintended impact of the call for balance on the length of management reports. The need to balance our short-term financial targets and longer-lead nonfinancial goals—goals in areas like customer satisfaction, process efficiency, and skills development—does not translate into a need for intricately balanced performance reports. If we limit what we report to the indicators that test key strategic assumptions, those reports will shorten dramatically. And they will do so by focusing only on what's relevant for the actions we propose to take.

A Relevant Definition

To clear up confusion about why we measure what we measure, we need to know what makes performance indicators relevant, and that means asking what it is to which they're relevant. The question is important enough that it's worth putting in terms so ugly they're hard to forget. What does knowing what matters require? It requires knowing *to what what matters matters.*

Suppose you're trying to decide between two possible measures of your mortgage processing team's productivity. You could focus on the average time spent processing a loan application or the average payroll cost per application. The first measure is sensitive to the efficiency of a given team, while the second is sensitive to the efficiency of teams with different payroll expenses. Which measure is more relevant?

You can't really say without deciding what it is to which metrics are supposed to be relevant in the first place. Most people who have written about performance measures seem to define relevance with respect to types of businesses, types of problems, or types of solutions. If they're really relevant to types of businesses, for example, then you'd expect the same metrics to be relevant to every mortgage loan processor. If they're really relevant to types of business problems, such as raising productivity, then you'd expect the same metrics to be relevant to every manager trying to raise productivity. And if they're really relevant to types of solutions to problems, like matching staff to loans, then you'd expect the same metrics to be relevant to every manager pursuing a similar strategy.

There's a big difference, however, between relevance to solutions and relevance to business types or problems. Relevance to business types or problems is judgmental. It's hard to imagine two competitors in the same business agreeing on the right things to measure, and it's not much easier imagining two managers faced with the same problem agreeing on performance indicators either. For example, if you try to increase mortgage processing productivity by matching staff experience levels to types of loans, you may want to measure time per loan. A competitor who tries to solve the productivity problem by changing the mix of experience levels, however, will want to measure cost per loan.

Relevance to solutions is startlingly different. Relevance to solutions really means relevance to an expectation or assumption about what will work. Unlike types of businesses or problems, expectations and assumptions are assertions. We can treat them as predictions. So any two people pursuing the same solution to a problem are basically making similar predictions about it. Since there's nothing judgmental about what is relevant to a prediction, they should agree on what's relevant and what isn't.

For instance, if you and a competitor both decide to try to raise productivity by giving complex loan applications to experienced staff and simple ones to inexperienced staff, then you're both making a similar assertion: that experience has a larger impact on processing complex loan applications than simple ones. No matter what else is different about your businesses or the specific productivity problems you face, you'll agree that time per loan is relevant to the strategy you're asserting. More specifically, it's relevant to the question whether the strategy is right.

The relevance of performance indicators to strategic assumptions and expectations is exceptionally clear. It's certainly clearer than relevance to business problems or even types of businesses. And that's a good reason to think that testing strategic assumptions may be the best use of performance reporting.

This view of performance reporting holds out real hope of finding the needles of information we need from the haystacks of data our systems thresh out. It basically says, "Derive performance metrics from your assumptions." It complements the eight-line strategies of Chapter Two since they focus on precisely the assumptions that need testing. And it suggests a concrete definition of relevance:

A performance indicator is relevant to a strategic assumption if the assumption's truth or falsity greatly affects the results you expect.

If the results from an indicator are equally likely whether your assumptions are true or false, then it is irrelevant.

Let's use the definition to see whether time per loan, as a performance indicator, is relevant to the assumption that matching staff experience levels to loan types will raise the productivity of a mortgage processing unit. Suppose you allocate complex loans to more experienced staff and then measure the group's average time per loan. You expect time per loan to fall. According to the definition, the metric is relevant if the assumption's falsity makes a drop in time per loan a lot more surprising. And it does. It's hard to imagine why time per loan would fall if matching staff experience levels and loan types had no effect on productivity.

Time per loan is irrelevant to other kinds of assumptions, however. Let's say you think you can increase productivity by hiring more inexperienced loan processors. You believe the cost savings in salary will make up for any extra time they take to process applications. In fact, you expect time per loan to rise a little.

But how surprising would a small rise in time per loan be if you somehow knew you were wrong about the assumption? You might have learned you were wrong from an independent study showing that the average salary of experienced loan processors offsets their efficiency. The problem is that a rise in time per loan is just as likely whether experienced workers are more cost-effective or less cost-effective in loan processing. To assumptions about cost-effectiveness, in other words, time per loan is irrelevant. In this case, you could probably tell right away that an indicator ignoring expenses was irrelevant to an assumption varying them. But often it's not obvious. In those cases, a clear definition of relevance is crucial.

Consider whether a single experience can be relevant to an assumption. It's true, for example, that the experience of a terrible hurricane season in 2005 was relevant to the assumption that the weather is getting more variable, and the definition shows why. Hurricane Katrina really tested that assumption. Its devastating effects would have been even more surprising if we were wrong about the weather growing unstable.

But that experience didn't test other assumptions we might well make—for example, that average temperatures are rising fast. The reason is that you can easily get a bad hurricane year even if average temperatures are constant. In other words, a bad hurricane wouldn't be all that surprising even if global warming were false and temperatures were just becoming more variable. It takes other kinds of evidence—like the decades of records we have been accumulating—to test global warming assumptions.

One advantage of this definition of relevance is that it shows how to think about the relevance of different kinds of performance results to a strategic assumption. Moreover, it shows how we can actually compete on the relevance of our results to what we need to learn and understand about strategy.

To illustrate this, let me take one more example from Iraq. It may not seem at first like a good idea to take examples from a wrenching, ongoing experience on which we cannot yet have much perspective. The decision to invade Iraq was unusually unambiguous, however, and it drew unusually clear criticism of the assumptions behind it and the evidence that might have tested those assumptions. For both of these reasons, it's one of the best cases for understanding what makes evidence relevant to strategic assumptions that we're likely to see for a long time.

Consider whether North Atlantic Treaty Organization (NATO) experience in Serbia and Kosovo was relevant to the assumption that a change of regime would stabilize Iraq following an invasion. NATO efforts to pacify the Balkans culminated with a successful air campaign to protect Albanians in the Serbian province of Kosovo from ethnic cleansing by the Serbian army. Shortly after the campaign, a democratic election removed Slobodan Milosevic, who had directed the ethnic cleansing campaign, from power.

Many thought this result supported the belief that Iraq would stabilize once Saddam Hussein was out of power. The theory was that majorities, given an opportunity to live under democratic rule, would enforce peace and calm—even if a minority of extremists tried to disrupt it. The Balkan experience may even have seemed enough to justify an invasion removing Saddam from power.

According to the definition proposed here, however, it was irrelevant. Postconflict stability in the Balkans would have been no more surprising if the assumption that democracy could motivate majorities to enforce a peace were wrong. In the case of the Balkans, half a dozen new countries separated the ethnic groups that had competed for power. Those borders might well explain the stability that the Balkans started to enjoy at the turn of the century regardless of the impact of democracy. Because new borders largely separated combatants, in other words, the Balkan experience didn't test whether democracy will inspire majorities to enforce a peace without those borders.[5]

The value of the definition does not lie in second-guessing past decisions, however. Its value lies in the fact that you can apply it prospectively. Even before the invasion of Iraq, for example, you could have compared the relevance of experiences like the Kosovo war to the prospects for postinvasion Iraqi stability with likely adversaries' experience in places such as Kashmir, Chechnya, or Afghanistan. Asking just the question how surprising their experience would have been if their strategic assumptions were wrong, I've argued elsewhere that the lessons potential insurgents gleaned from Chechnya and Afghanistan were far more relevant to assumptions about postinvasion stability in Iraq than what U.S. planners learned from the Balkans and the first Gulf War.[6]

This definition lets you determine in advance whether the relevance of your past experience to some initiative puts you at an advantage or a disadvantage to possible competitors. Even more important is the relevance to the initiative of your organization's ongoing experience in the form of the kind of indicators you can measure.

This represents a real opportunity because you can create an advantage by thinking hard about what indicators you should watch to test your strategy. Even if you start with the same strategy as a competitor, a better choice of indicators can help you learn what works and improve it faster. The opportunity is all the greater because so few companies draw a clear connection between how they measure performance and whether their strategies are right.

Strategy or Dogma?

Whether they know it or not, most organizations use a definition of relevance that's starkly different from the one I set out in the previous section. Their performance metrics either ignore strategy altogether, track red herrings, or get lost in endless demands for more data. As a result, they tend to become less adaptable or mired in complexity.

The wealth of detail on actual balanced scorecards in Kaplan and Norton's *Strategy Maps* affords plenty of examples of performance metrics that for one reason or another don't test strategy. Media General's performance metrics (as of 2004) seemed to ignore its real strategy, for instance. Balanced scorecards at Saatchi & Saatchi seemed to chase red herrings. And Ingersoll Rand seemed trapped in the pursuit of ever more data. The performance of these companies—all participants at one point or another in Kaplan's and Norton's Balanced Scorecard Collaborative—has been no better or worse than most of their competitors'. So there was little compensation for the painful dilemmas between strategic stagnation and management complexity their use of balanced scorecards apparently created.

Media General is probably the most typical case. In their third book, Kaplan and Norton present what they call a strategy map for the publisher—a picture of causal relations among the performance goals that arguably belong on its scorecard.[7] The Media General scorecard is a model of balance. The only problem is that it doesn't reflect what seems to have been the company's real strategy.

Let's start with what it does reflect. Media General's strategy map and associated high-level scorecard are most detailed about performance goals for internal processes. They include the product-oriented goals of creating and acquiring new products and services and developing and delivering better content. They include the audience-oriented goals of expanding circulation, viewership, and users; building strong community partnerships; and enhancing public trust and identity. And they include the advertiser-oriented goals of providing "innovative multimedia/ multimarket content and sales," continuously improving service quality, and winning new advertisers and gaining market share from existing accounts.[8]

This list is so comprehensive that it's hard to imagine what isn't in it. It has echoes of the teacher's pet who, when asked what she wants to improve, tells her enraptured instructor, "Everything, Mr. Peabody. I want to get better at everything."

These internal process goals are supposed to lead to five performance goals from a customer perspective. You can think of them as Media General's value proposition for both media consumers and advertisers. The firm promises media consumers accurate, compelling, and relevant content, as well as integrity, fairness, and objectivity in delivering that content. It promises advertisers that it will deliver the audiences they desire and provide quality service. And it assures all stakeholders of its ongoing community involvement.[9]

They are, once again, all worthy aspirations. Readers of some of Media General's newspapers admittedly may raise their eyebrows at the goal of "fairness and objectivity." The bland pursuit of unobjectionable news stories scrubbed of any identifiable point of view is not one of the faults of the *Richmond Times-Dispatch,* for example. In fact, several Media General publications are throwbacks to the days when papers could rely on their readers to disentangle facts from editorial viewpoints.

The point is that four of these five customer-oriented performance goals could fit in any media company's balanced scorecard. They reveal nothing precise about how Media General hoped to compete in a tough market. The only goal that shows a little personality is the one about community involvement. But while it begins to hint at what was distinctive in Media General's approach, you can hardly call it a strategy.

For a clearer picture of what Media General's strategy may really have been, take a look at what some of its critics had to say. Referring to Media General and a handful of other regionally focused media companies with a conservative editorial perspective, Robert McChesney, the founder of the independent media advocacy group Free Press, claimed, "Their vision is of owning an empire of company media towns with one monopoly newsroom servicing all the outlets in a town, and a massive reliance on inexpensive syndicated fare."[10] Now that looks like a strategy.

In their case study of Media General, Kaplan and Norton describe the company's market focus. It's interesting in this age of global communication that Media General set itself a regional target: the southeastern United States. Within that target market, explained CEO Stewart Bryan, Media General pursued what he called convergence to "coordinate different media in a given market to provide quality information in the way each does best—but delivered from a comprehensive and unified perspective."[11] The idea was to be a primary source of newspaper, television, and online information services in each local market where it operated.

The two parts of the strategy would work together. Although southeastern U.S. media markets are hardly homogeneous, they include some of the highest concentrations of politically like-minded media consumers in the country. That would help garner community support for the firm's local newspaper, television, and Internet cross-holdings. Those local cross-holdings, in turn, would create scale economies in the production of content and advertising and leverage in negotiations with advertisers.

What I've just listed, of course, are key assumptions for the strategy of a company like Media General. And yet they went mostly untested in the firm's balanced scorecard. That scorecard included a lot of good stuff, but it didn't include indicators for the kind of assumptions that could support a specific strategy.

You might argue that time had already tested those assumptions. By 2004, surely, they fell into the category of "settled assumptions" that an eight-line strategy can skip. But the assumption of something like community support for a locally dominant media firm—even one with a congenial point of view—is constantly vulnerable to change. And the belief that advertisers, including political ones, will prefer the convenience of one-stop shopping to the benefits of competitive bargaining will always require review.

Even if it's fair to conclude that the company's scorecard reflected little of its real strategy—and bear in mind that you always have to read between the lines to draw a conclusion like this—Media General is hardly unusual. Simply put, most firms think of performance management as a kind of hygiene unrelated to strategy—even with influential authors like Kaplan and Norton in the market urging otherwise.

Such a disconnection between strategy and performance reporting can be dangerous. Your performance is often the earliest warning you could possibly have that something is wrong with your strategy—but only if you test it.

McChesney gives an example of what can go wrong, especially if you don't check up on strategy through your performance management system: "In 2003, when [former Federal Communications Commission chairman] Powell tried to eliminate any restrictions on local media ownership, the public revolted, with an extraordinary left-right coalition that generated nearly 3 million letters."[12] Unhappy with the rising cost of media time in the past few elections, moreover, U.S. politicians from both parties have started to complain. Media companies relying on local concentration strategies need to test public sentiment constantly about their cross-holdings. It's hard to imagine what higher purpose performance reporting can really serve than that kind of test.

Red Herrings

Not all performance reporting systems ignore actual strategy, of course. Those that do try to test strategy, however, tend to fall into one of two other traps. Some track red herrings to try to confirm their strategy; others try to capture strategy through the relentless measurement of more and more of its operational requirements. The advertising firm Saatchi & Saatchi looks like an example of the former and the industrial conglomerate Ingersoll Rand an example of the latter.

In 1997, new Saatchi & Saatchi CEO Kevin Roberts and new CFO Bill Cochrane introduced the strategy and sole customer-oriented performance goal of creating "permanently infatuated clients."[13] The resulting balanced scorecard gives a real jolt. The performance goal from a customer perspective was not only undiluted but also quite specific. Clients were to be not merely satisfied but infatuated, with the dimension of being pleased beyond reason (and perhaps even incapable of rational fee negotiation). Not only were they to be infatuated for a day or so, but permanently.

This is a strategy you could test. How many clients are infatuated enough to return telephone calls quickly? Are they infatuated enough to expand their accounts? And are they sufficiently infatuated to keep doing so week after week? It's not clear how strenuously Roberts and Cochrane tested their success in durably infatuating clients or whether they tested it at all. But their balanced scorecard made clear what sorts of process performance goals were supposed to lead to this outcome.

The scorecard's strategy map gives six performance goals from an internal process perspective designed to deliver seriously pleased customers. They include the productivity goals of eliminating inefficiencies and "working smarter" across the network; the general quality goal of excelling at account management and creating great ads; the marketing goals of focusing business development and identifying and implementing appropriate communication services; and the general branding goal of winning "global fame for . . . idea leadership."[14]

At first sight, these process performance goals may seem similar to those of Media General: prescriptions for good business practice but hardly a strategy for achieving something specific like creating infatuated clients. That's certainly true of the goals for efficiency, network cooperation, and communication services. Two of the other process goals start to point at a more specific and distinctive program, however, and the third at least provides an idea for measuring a component of client infatuation.

Powering the goal of creating great ads were proposals (unfortunately called "Big, Fabulous Ideas") to transform the positioning of client products. An example would be using Pepcid to prevent heartburn rather than just to relieve it.[15] Product repositioning goes beyond the aspiration of many advertising agencies and could represent a way to create strong client loyalty.

Similarly, while the goal of focusing business development sounds like a bromide, it meant something quite specific: executives must make clear business cases to invest in developing new clients. The effect of this internal process goal was to focus attention on delighting and retaining existing clients rather than chasing new prospects.

Finally, the goal of winning fame for idea leadership tested a strategic assumption. To find out whether great product repositioning ideas have the power to infatuate clients, you need an independent measure of how great the ideas are. Fame might provide it.

In short, the scorecard articulated a distinctive value proposition and several processes related to it. Ultimately, however, even the edgier process performance goals back away from testing a specific way to create permanently infatuated clients. Success against these goals, as stated, might have reflected executives' efforts to reposition major products of existing clients. But they might have reflected the execution of a wealth of alternative strategies as well.

Such goals are red herrings in that they don't fully test the strategy behind them. You can see that they are red herrings by applying the definition at the beginning of the chapter. Just ask whether a successful result against the goals as stated would have been any more surprising if you knew the repositioning strategy could not work.

Suppose the company succeeded in each of its operational goals as they're stated and managed to infatuate its clients too. That means, among other things, it would have created great ads. But it's easy to imagine the company creating great ads out of very small ideas that had nothing to do with their clients' product positioning.

By the same token, you can imagine the company winning fame—or notoriety—for idea leadership without ever developing a big, positive idea for a client. Ads attacking its clients' competitors with enough gusto and flare could do the trick. The firm could have reaped commercial rewards in this case too—from clients worried how they would appear in Saatchi & Saatchi ads for a competitor if they let their accounts lapse. But this would have been the very different strategy of creating permanently intimidated clients.

To sum up, Saatchi & Saatchi could have succeeded in its operating goals even if its strategy of focusing on big ideas such as product repositioning for existing clients were infeasible. The six goals listed above test lots of good business practices, but they don't test whether you can compete by reliably generating frame-breaking ideas. You would need a goal specifying the kind of great ads that the strategy targets to do that.

It may seem that I'm asking for too much here. Kaplan and Norton point out that Roberts and Cochrane quintupled the firm's shareholder value in the three years they ran it before selling it to Publicis Group S.A. in 2000. "This dramatic performance earned Saatchi & Saatchi membership in the Balanced Scorecard Hall of Fame," they add.[16] But understanding the strategy that leads to success is crucial if you hope to repeat or improve on that success. Besides, the firm was a wreck in 1997.

Charles and Maurice Saatchi emigrated from Baghdad's Jewish community as toddlers in 1947. They started the advertising company bearing their names in 1970 and went on an acquisition binge, spraying $1 billion around the world in sixteen years to buy thirty-seven agencies. By 1986, they had five hundred offices in sixty-five countries. According to *Conflicting Accounts* author Kevin Goldman, however, they spent no time on integration.[17]

Charles apparently rarely attended a meeting of the board even though he was its chairman. Instead, he focused on London's art scene, building a celebrated gallery and cultivating the generation of Young British Artists. Among the creative talents he patronized were Jake and Dinos Chapman, who stunned art lovers around the world in 2003 by publicly defacing a mint-condition set of Goya's astonishing eighty-print series *The Disasters of War* that they had bought (it helps to have rich patrons) two years earlier.[18] Their big idea was to paint meticulous clown faces and puppy dog heads over the visages of Goya's mutilated cadavers, including those hanging from trees.

Maurice focused on key clients until 1994, when the board rejected a fat stock option package he had awarded himself despite years of financial losses and ousted him. Forming a new firm called M&C Saatchi, he and Charles battled their old company after investors sold it to Cordiant Communications. The markets have forced the Saatchi brothers to improve on their earlier strategy: the new firm built its sixteen current offices around the world from scratch rather than through hard-to-integrate acquisitions.

Cordiant spun off the struggling network in 1997 and brought in Roberts and Cochrane to run it. It's not clear their turnaround success supports balanced scorecards because they had the advantage of starting from a low base. That a performance tool improved this firm's management in 1997 does not make it noteworthy in itself.

Moreover, it's not even clear that the strategy supposedly reflected in Saatchi & Saatchi's balanced scorecard explains the success the firm has enjoyed. Results have remained in line with the industry even though the strategy has metamorphosed since Publicis bought it. Worse still for the claim that a balanced scorecard contributed to the company's success is the fact that the new strategy satisfies the scorecard's internal process objectives as well as the old one. The scorecard is strategy independent.

The new strategy is Lovemarks. You can think of them as the brand of Kevin Roberts. Now in his tenth year as CEO of Saatchi & Saatchi, he has written two books on the concept.[19] Lovemarks are brands that inspire loyalty beyond reason. They should sound familiar because the firm's strategy before 2000 was to inspire loyalty beyond reason. But the difference is that he now sells this strategy to clients.

To the extent Roberts has succeeded in fueling further Saatchi & Saatchi growth with Lovemarks, he has transformed his own company's strategy from one of infatuating clients into one of pitching and mass-customizing a cool new brand concept. Whatever they feel about Saatchi & Saatchi, clients now need to be infatuated with Lovemarks.

The new strategy confirms a weakness in the old Saatchi & Saatchi scorecard. Its internal process performance goals don't distinguish between the old strategy of infatuating clients with the firm and the new one of pitching infatuation as a brand concept for clients. That's obviously true of the four goals for efficiency, network cooperation, communications services, and idea leadership. It's equally true of the goal of creating great ads, since ads that serve to infatuate clients and ads that infatuate clients' customers can both be great. And it's true of the goal of focusing business development since both strategies can emphasize renewing existing accounts.

So the Saatchi & Saatchi balanced scorecard is sufficiently general to cover distinct strategies. As a result, it fails to test which one you're implementing, and therefore its measures are irrelevant to the question of whether a particular strategy is succeeding as intended.

This may explain why, despite the discipline of a scorecard to spell out how the firm would achieve success, Saatchi & Saatchi under Roberts has lurched from one strategy to another. Strategy must evolve for a firm to grow. But the switchback at Saatchi & Saatchi makes its strategic development seem incoherent. You get the impression that at this masterful spinner of promotional strategies, the company's own strategies are just-so stories. Saatchi & Saatchi competes for talent and serves its clients like other agencies. It just tells better stories about what works.

A final irony is that the Saatchi brothers have also built their strategy around a brand concept, which they call Brutal Simplicity. It emphasizes one-word brands and brand equity, both of which seem to require a certain brutality of language. You might say that the brothers are selling Hate while Roberts is selling Love. But they're both pursuing similar strategies today.

The Search for Universal Data

Against the standard of testing a specific strategy, then, Saatchi & Saatchi measured red herrings. Its performance measures were irrelevant to the question of whether its strategy was succeeding as planned. Equipment manufacturer Ingersoll Rand, however, seems to be trying to capture its strategy on a balanced scorecard through the relentless measurement of all possible operational requirements. It's as if the managers were trying through brute force to harmonize the firm's twin commitments to strategy renewal and the measurement of all aspects of performance.

You can see this in the balanced scorecard and strategy map that Ingersoll Rand rolled out to transform its strategy in 1999. New CEO Herb Henkel needed to raise the company's share price performance above the slow-growth level of branded equipment manufacturers. He decided to turn the venerable manufacturer of a portfolio of locks, refrigeration equipment, electric vehicles, and construction and mining equipment into a provider of integrated solutions for its industrial clients.

That strategy may not be apparent in two of the scorecard's three customer-perspective goals. You don't have to be a solutions provider to want to "provide the best products, services, and solutions" and "create loyalty through excellence in quality, service, and delivery." But it's clear from the third goal, which is to "develop partnerships to deliver the best total value."[20] The idea is to find the right balance of product features, services, and price for each customer.

Solutions strategies are hardly unique. Ever since Lou Gerstner made over IBM as a solutions provider, the strategy has grown increasingly popular among manufacturers and technology companies. It's certainly more common than the shift in the other direction, from solutions to products. That, you could argue, is the path Saatchi & Saatchi has taken by focusing on a particular brand concept after basically selling itself. But firms that have moved from providing solutions to selling products are in the minority.

Although they're not unique, solutions strategies are explicit. A solutions provider generally does not try to provide best-in-class products, cheapest prices, or distinctive services. Solutions providers are good at rebalancing the mix of product attributes, service quality, and pricing for each client.

The Ingersoll Rand scorecard fails to show clearly how to transform into a solutions provider. Take a look at its three high-level process goals:

- Drive dramatic growth through innovation.
- Drive demand through customer/end-user intimacy.
- Drive operational excellence.[21]

The goal for operational excellence is about continuous improvement and turns out to be quite interesting. The other two, however, seem to conflict. Which will it be? Growing demand through an intimate knowledge of the combination of features, services, and price each customer prefers? Or accelerating growth through product leadership? If you're tempted to try to combine the two goals into a strategy that builds customer intimacy through product leadership, just think what kind of marketers you would hire. Are they supposed to be relationship managers or product advocates? It's hard to have it both ways. Solutions providers must be ready to opt dispassionately for another company's product if it will fit into a better overall solution for a customer.

Henkel's team seemed to sense a problem here and tried to solve it by moving to a higher level of detail even in the conglomerate's top-level strategy map. Under the goal of growth through innovation, for example, the scorecard calls for managing the product portfolio for competitive advantage; restructuring businesses and markets for growth and profitability; acquiring complementary solutions; developing differentiated applications and solutions; and targeting growth markets and segments.

The goal of driving demand through "customer/end-user intimacy" breaks into leveraging Ingersoll Rand's channel and customer network; broadly understanding customer and end-user needs; customizing marketing programs for key clients; targeting high-priority channels; and aligning with the "market-driving" customers in each targeted channel. Under the goal of driving operational excellence, finally, fall the continuous improvement of health, safety, and environmental practices; the continuous improvement of manufacturing network efficiency and effectiveness; the creation of a best-in-class corporate center; the creation of similarly best-in-class corporate center processes and services; a design emphasis on speed, cost, and value; and the continuous improvement of technology, efficiency, and effectiveness in all major corporate processes.[22]

You might have expected that the higher resolution of a list of more detailed goals could help pick out a specific route to becoming a solutions provider. It's certainly an interesting list. Yet instead of resolving the tension between product innovation and customer intimacy goals, it just defers the conflict to the next level of detail. Worse still, things are beginning to get complicated. If this is what top management's scorecard looked like in 2000, imagine what operating managers had to juggle.

At first sight, the goal of developing differentiated applications and solutions appears to narrow the firm's aspiration for innovation to a specific means—unique solutions—of promoting customer intimacy. Alongside it, however, are two other goals that broaden the innovation aspiration right back again into full conflict with a true solutions strategy. The goal of managing the product portfolio for competitive advantage focuses on the company's own products. Solutions may involve whatever a customer needs, it seems to say, so long as we make the main bits and pieces.

Even more jarring, given the strategy of transforming the company into a solutions provider, is the goal of acquiring complementary solutions. If it were just a matter of acquiring the best available components from any source for a given customer solution, it would be fine. But that's not what it means.

Ingersoll Rand completed sixty acquisitions between 2000 and 2005.[23] The market appeared to be confused about Henkel's strategy and became impatient for growth. Acquisitions provide growth, even if they defer its costs. So Henkel bought a lot of firms. The merger spree was probably no surprise. Henkel had acquired seventeen companies as president of Textron's Industrial Products unit between 1993 and 1998.

Acquisition programs don't have to be bad news. They're disturbing, though, in the context of a solutions strategy. A solutions provider does not need to own the companies that make the components of the systems it assembles. Most corporate acquisitions, furthermore, command a 30 percent premium to their market price. By combining an acquisition program and a solutions strategy, Ingersoll Rand seemed to doom itself to providing solutions at a 30 percent premium to what its customers might have procured on their own.

Concerns about integrating all of those acquisitions and a share price-earnings ratio stuck below the average for the firm's industry apparently touched a nerve. In a 2006 interview, Henkel lamented, "We never receive the recognition we deserve. It's vital to craft an image of a well-integrated company, and branding is a big part of this."[24] The reporter helpfully noted that strategic branding consultants Siegel & Gale advised Ingersoll Rand to remove the hyphen from its name. Perhaps the consultants thought that the hyphen was giving away the integration challenge the company faces.

Together with its customer intimacy objectives, then, the product portfolio and solution acquisition goals on its scorecard commit Ingersoll Rand to doing two different things: building great products and customizing client solutions. In other words, the scorecard does not reflect a single strategy. It does, however, shed some light on why organizations embrace performance goals that create complexity without picking out a specific strategy.

Many organizations using balanced scorecards seem to seek a universal list of requirements for success. If they know everything about their performance, runs the apparent logic, at least part of what they know will be what really matters.

Look back at Ingersoll Rand's process goals. It's a worthy set of aspirations. With the possible exception of the solution acquisition goal, and recognizing that they may aim at two conflicting strategies, these sixteen process objectives comprise a decent list of what various kinds of success at Ingersoll Rand would require.

There's something appealingly virtuous about a list of requirements. It reminds you of the disciplines you should never forget. You won't succeed without curbing costs, for example, so keep costs down. You won't succeed without listening to customers, either, so invite feedback. And so forth. Herb Henkel is an admirable spokesman for this kind of discipline. He quotes his grandfather's adage that "you don't have to be bad to do better."[25] It's a reminder that there's always something to learn. This idea of continuous improvement is a powerful element of the Ingersoll Rand scorecard.

Performance measures have the potential to let you do something you could never do without them, however. The real-world results they report can show whether you're right about how to achieve success. More precisely, their results can reveal flaws in your theory about what works. And this is something lists of requirements cannot do.

It's true that lists of requirements in the form of performance goals can show when you're way off track, but they cannot test the validity of your ideas about how to succeed. The reason is simple. We're almost never wrong about requirements. Where we're often wrong is about how to get something done. For the logicians in the audience, requirements are necessary conditions for success. Strategies are sufficient conditions.

A list of requirements for making a soufflé might include proportions of eggs, flour, milk, and butter; a soufflé dish; and an oven. Anybody can eventually figure out, by inspecting the final product, what a soufflé requires. But very few people can write out a reliable recipe for producing a good soufflé. A list of requirements is not a recipe.

When it comes to organizational success as opposed to soufflés, moreover, there's no end to the requirements. The four volumes

Kaplan and Norton have produced on balanced scorecards are eloquent testimony to this. Each volume breaks the categories of performance goals—or requirements for success—into finer subcategories. Balanced scorecards invite a search for universal data about how we're doing, as if, at some level of detail, those data eventually might capture individual strategies in their net. And yet no list of ingredients, however detailed, could ever tell you how to prepare a soufflé.

This is a bit unfair as a blanket condemnation of balanced scorecards since some of them do specify testable strategies. But when they do, they seem to do so by accident.

The comparison of scorecards with lists of requirements, moreover, puts the uses that Ingersoll Rand and Saatchi & Saatchi made of balanced scorecards in perspective. Both companies tried to connect the performance measures in their scorecards to their strategies. And both satisfied themselves with, at best, indirect connections. They differed in their views—both wrong, in my opinion—of finding data to support decisions.

Saatchi & Saatchi was overly optimistic about finding data to support strategic decisions. Its managers seemed to believe that any performance result that was consistent with its strategic assumptions supported them. Success against the process goal of creating great ads, for example, was consistent with infatuating clients. It was also consistent with the strategy of pitching a specific brand concept like Lovemarks. You could reverse the strategy and keep the same scorecard!

But the fact that a performance result is consistent with a strategic assumption doesn't mean it's relevant to the assumption. A 10 percent rise in sales may be consistent with the installation of a complicated enterprise planning system, for example. And yet if we believe the rise would have been just as likely without the enterprise planning system, we can't use the rise in sales to justify the installation.

Ingersoll Rand was overly pessimistic about finding data to support strategic decisions. Its managers seemed to think only results that proved their assumptions were relevant to them. The scorecard's five customer intimacy objectives were apparently not enough to test the firm's new solutions strategy, so they added a raft of product innovation goals that really belong to a different strategy.

Asking performance metrics to prove a strategic assumption, however, is much too harsh. For one thing, plenty of metrics can show an assumption is wrong even if they could never prove it. Regional sales figures could never prove that a local advertising pilot is effective, for example, because you can never hold constant everything else that distinguishes your sales regions. They can nevertheless go a long way toward convincing you that a pilot has had no impact.

Another reason you shouldn't expect performance measures to prove your strategic assumptions is that the strongest assumptions are sweeping in scope. But if they're sweeping in scope, they should be hard or impossible to prove. For instance, the assumption that client service is more important than product features in all of a given product's markets is powerful. It may also be wrong. But how would you ever prove it beyond a doubt?

What I'm saying is that both of these views—overoptimism and overpessimism about finding data to support strategic decisions—misconstrue what it takes for a performance measure to be relevant to a strategy. The definition of relevance at the beginning of the chapter offers a middle way. Let's see how it works.

4

KEY PERFORMANCE INDICATORS AND THE METRICS MATRIX

This civilization has not yet fully recovered
from the shock of its birth—the transition from
the tribal or closed society, with its submission to
magical forces, to the open society which sets free
the critical powers of man.

—*Karl Popper*

With his moustache and goatee, Mike Rowen looked the part of the tenacious new product champion. At credit card innovator Capital One, of course, it was the tenacity, not the looks, that counted. So when investors pressed the company to build an Internet presence in 1999, it made sense to ask Mike to spearhead the effort.[1]

As is usually the case at Capital One, Rowen led with a hypothesis. He reasoned that online accounts would tend to come from early technology adopters. And he hypothesized that these early technology adopters would tend to be better credits.

The trouble was that there were no metrics at hand to test the assumption. Specifically, there was no way in 1999 to check the relationship of credit scores and income demographics to credit card charge-offs for people trying to open accounts online. Capital One would have to make a bet and keep an eye on how credit problems developed among their new online accounts.

During the program's first year in that frothy economy, things did not deteriorate too quickly. But by the end of the year, Rowen's team could start to see a difference between what they would have expected from similar offline accounts and what they were getting from their online accounts. They had hoped for positive selection: technology-savvy users looking for convenience. They were getting adverse selection: people whose offline credit applications had not passed other banks' screens. Two years and one and a half million accounts later, with annualized bad debt charges on the order of $20 million a year, Capital One exited the business.

In retrospect, it all seems so obvious, but it wasn't at the time. After all, there was plenty of evidence that early online users were reliable. eBay was having good experience with its early adopters, for example. In fact, the big news in the late 1990s was how few bad credit and transaction problems were muddying early Web commerce.

Evidence that might support its working hypothesis wasn't what Capital One needed, however. What it needed was evidence that had the potential to overturn its hypothesis. The lesson is so important that chief credit officer (and executive vice president) Peter Schnall bakes it into his decision making training for Capital One executives. He warns his students passionately against the confirming evidence trap.

In a classic article, "The Hidden Traps in Decision Making," John Hammond, Ralph Keeney, and Howard Raiffa define the confirming evidence trap as "seeking information that supports your existing point of view."[2] They cite a psychological experiment that asked its participants to read two careful studies. One reached the conclusion that the death penalty is effective, and the other concluded it is not. All participants emerged more strongly convinced of their ingoing opinions. In other words, they paid attention only to the evidence that confirmed their view.

It's obvious why people look for confirming evidence: we want to be right. What's not so obvious is why this is a trap: adverse evidence has far greater power than confirming evidence. As Karl Popper argued in book after book, confirming evidence can never prove a theory, while adverse evidence can conclusively refute it.[3] For example, evidence that online customers tend to be good credit risks—and even early evidence that your own customers are good credit risks—can never prove they will be good credit risks through a business cycle. But just a quarter's experience of credit that's worse than you expected will show that the reasoning behind your expectations was wrong.

By 2005, the credit card industry's falling acceptance rates from mail offers convinced Capital One to take another look at the online market. This time, a smart, funny, unassuming twenty-six-year-old Cornell engineer from Colombia named Andreas Vives was responsible. As before, his team started with a hypothesis: online applicants now were savvy buyers shopping for economic offers. These are just the customers Capital One wants to serve. And this time the team could test their assumption.

Vives's analysts armed themselves with three stages of metrics to monitor the quality of the online credit portfolio. They modeled expected charge-offs based on the features of their product offers, the income demographics and credit scores of their online credit applications, and their cardholders' three-month and six-month experience.

The team also deployed a strikingly simple metric that provided a perspective over and above its three-stage credit model. The Web site asked online credit applicants to grade their own credit quality and select a product from a range of offerings aimed at different levels of credit risk. Capital One might not give applicants what they requested, but the responses added a valuable dimension to the team's analysis.

Metrics tracking applicants' self-grading and product self-selection have proven surprisingly powerful. Rates of deliberate fraud or misrepresentation are never zero but are often not high. Customers will tell you what they think of their own credit quality if you give them a chance. In the process, they will reveal whether they are truly savvy buyers, as Vives's team assumed. They might even have helped Rowen's team avoid the confirming evidence trap six years earlier. This time around, Capital One's Internet pool has been profitable for two years and has performed as well as comparable pools.

In a new book on business analytics, Tom Davenport and Jeanne Harris boil the active ingredient in Capital One's approach down to what CEO and founder Rich Fairbank calls an "information-based strategy."[4] But that's like saying Tiger Woods's golf game rests on an air-based strategy. It might be truer to say that Tiger Woods succeeds despite air and Capital One succeeds despite (too much) information.

Capital One uses its hypotheses to narrow the focus of any problem-solving team to manageable proportions. But it doesn't trust those hypotheses; it tests them and remembers what it learns. You might say that the information so vital to Fairbank is the product of its strategy rather than the key ingredient. Davenport and Harris hint as much when they conclude, "Few companies are truly set up to apply the principles of this test-and-learn approach, but Capital One's entire distinctive capability is built on it."[5] The point is that testing and learning do not start with data. They start with assumptions. The information Capital One piles up by the terabyte is what it learns from testing them.

Capital One is an example of an adaptive company that derives performance metrics from key assumptions. In fact, its teams go further. To avoid the confirming evidence trap, they look for metrics that might overthrow their assumptions. Toyota also sees assumption-driven metrics as a requirement for adaptability. In fact, the hunt for measures to check and throw doubt on plans at every level of the firm seems to be part of its culture. You might call it enterprisewide fallibilism.

Matt May puts it a little differently in his recent book on innovation at Toyota.[6] He calls it perfectionism and traces it to the principles of firm founder Kiichiro Toyoda.[7] Toyota Motor Sales U.S.A. hired May to translate the principles of the Toyota production system for nonproduction workers. He describes the Japanese version of continuous improvement called kaizen, for example, as repeatedly setting the highest possible standard for whatever you're doing and then experimenting until you find a way to beat the standard. Perfectionism is a rosier way of putting this than fallibilism. But I wonder whether it really gets at Toyota's cultural approach to performance management.

Toyota Motor Sales's vice president of finance and business planning, Rich Valenstein, shifts the emphasis when he reflects, "There is no best, only better."[8] In other words, perfection may be the goal, but we can never hope to get there and probably wouldn't recognize it if we stumbled across it by accident.

The first hint of this cultural leitmotif for Rich was his job interview with Jim Press, the president of Toyota Motor Sales at the time. "Why do you want to bring me on board?" Rich asked in all modesty, despite his background in Ford's vaunted finance group.

"We don't focus on what we're doing right," Press replied.

Like May, Rich puts a continuous improvement ethic at the heart of Toyota's problem-solving approach. Specifically, he credits Edward Deming's "plan, do, check, act" learning loop, which Toyota employees shorten to PDCA, and use as a verb. When colleagues found a missing reserve adjustment in one brand's preliminary February 2007 numbers, for example, the immediate response was, "Let's PDCA that."

It's easy to think you might instill the company's pervasive problem-solving attitude through a mix of disciplined management and effective motivation. Training and incentives might get an entire workforce to reach for the elegant solutions May describes instead of the obvious ones that might satisfy competitors. But it's not clear any amount of training and motivation could transplant the cultural attitude Rich describes when he says, "Whatever we're doing, regardless of success, it's not good enough." It's the kind of mind-set you might just have to coach, coax, and develop employee by employee.

This attitude has an immediate impact on the performance measures you use. As Rich puts it, if Toyota enjoys a higher loyalty rating than GM and Ford, then attention shifts to customer engagement. An increase in sales to former Hyundai owners shifts attention to former Toyota owners. In a nutshell, the right metric is the one that casts the most doubt on your current standard, plan, or assumptions.

You may wonder why I'm attributing Toyota's focus on plan-probing metrics to fallibilism instead of something more concrete like a problem-seeking culture.[9] That's not a bad term but it misses the active element of continuous planning. At the same time that Toyota employees look for problems—the C in PDCA—they make new proposals—the P in PDCA. No sooner do you find a brand or engineering problem than you make a plan about how you think you can better market your brand or assemble your chassis. And no sooner do you make a plan than you start looking for its shortcomings.

It's just not nature's way for us to get things perfectly right; we're all fallible, from the CEO to the mail clerk. So it's smart to expect imperfections in what you do and expose the inevitable next problem. Fallibilism doesn't encourage imperfection, but it stands for the idea that you'll keep learning only if you expect it.

This perspective provides an important contrast with the description of GE in Chapter One. GE puts the voice of the customer at the heart of its goal setting. Customer voice is important at Toyota too. But what if the customer's standard for whatever you're doing isn't the highest one you can imagine?

The point is not to goldplate products beyond what customers really need. It's a little more subtle. The point is that customers can be fallible too. It may be that your customers don't need better gas mileage today, but they just might in the future.

Both Toyota's ingrained fallibilism and Capital One's use of data to attack its hypotheses ensure that they measure what's relevant. Capital One measures what's relevant to its hypotheses by focusing on what might disprove them. Toyota measures what's relevant to its kaizen-generated standards or its PDCA-generated plans by focusing on what could reveal serious imperfections in them. In other words, they focus on indicators that are relevant to their assumptions—in strategy as well as operations.

Even at this level of generality, the contrast with the companies described in Chapter Three that leave assumptions untested, chase red herrings, or crank out unending lists of universal requirements is sharp. Let's take these three sins of irrelevance in turn.

To begin, neither Toyota nor Capital One holds any tenet of strategy sacrosanct; their performance measures challenge operating and strategic assumptions alike. Toyota once was a purely Japanese company, for example, but then PDCA'd the idea of opening U.S. plants. It was once a small-car firm but then PDCA'd sports utility vehicles. Capital One similarly tested—and passed—the ideas of making auto loans and extending health care finance. Of course, it took both organizations a while to test their new strategic assumptions, but that doesn't mean they hesitated to challenge the old ones.

Second, Toyota's culture protects it from the red herrings that distract other companies. By red herrings, I mean not just irrelevant performance indicators in general but the kind of indicators that seem to support a strategic assumption without really testing it. The example from Chapter Three was about whether the evidence supported the strategy of infatuating clients with your business itself as opposed to your specific offerings. Toyota's fallibilism immediately raises doubts whether any adopted strategy is best. The first thing a Toyota manager does with a new strategy is to collect indicators probing its flaws.

Finally, even supernumerate Capital One avoids the trap of looking for universal data. It's true that it seems as close as anyone else to collecting such a thing—at least when it comes to credit card users. But it doesn't look for it. There is no set of universal metrics in Capital One's data banks that can answer any question. Capital One teams look for whatever will test a specific hypothesis. You can think of that hypothesis as a pair of headlights cutting through the fog of irrelevant data. Data are the output.

This chapter wraps up the argument that learning from experience in an age of irrelevant information requires a new approach to performance metrics. It shows how to derive performance metrics from key assumptions, not from balanced lists of outputs and input requirements, as most scorecard applications seem to do.

The idea of deriving performance indicators from key assumptions promises a dramatic simplification of your planning and performance system. But to realize that promise, you need to tell which metrics are most relevant to your assumptions. The following sections introduce the metrics matrix, a tool to help you determine which indicators best test each of your key assumptions from an eight-line strategy. It can help you scrape the barnacles off your balanced scorecard and get it sailing again.

Far from being another analytical engine, the metrics matrix requires only a pen and piece of paper. There are three steps in using it:

1. Screening any set of performance metrics for relevance to your key strategic assumptions
2. Screening them for specificity and combining the screens to eliminate all but the most powerful metric for testing each assumption
3. Finding metrics for key untested assumptions

The first section shows how to rank any set of performance metrics for their relevance to a strategic assumption. This step turns out to be the crucial requirement for paring down your performance dashboard, scorecard, or management report until it's no longer than your list of critical unsettled assumptions. The second section shows how to rank any set of performance metrics for specificity. Coupled with the use of eight-line strategies from Chapter Two, the two rankings give you a performance dashboard of up to eight indicators.

In fact, the first two sections may simplify your performance dashboard too much. There's always a chance that no metric in your current management reports adequately tests one of your key unsettled assumptions. The third section therefore proposes some rules of thumb for constructing better metrics. What's distinctive here is a way of developing metrics from the logic of your assumptions.

The final section circles back to the question why such a simple approach to metrics selection could possibly work. It shows how the metrics matrix combines just the right parts of Bayesian probability, or the theory of how evidence affects beliefs, and information theory, the study of how messages reduce what we don't know about a situation, in an entirely intuitive tool. The section finishes with an effort to generalize the explanation in Chapter Three of why, for all their advantages, balanced scorecards rarely test strategies. They have a natural tendency to test something quite different: requirements for success. The problem, once again, is that we rarely mistake requirements but often pursue the wrong strategy. By testing something that is rarely wrong, balanced scorecards can lull us into a dangerous sense of infallibility.

Screening Indicators for Relevance

To test a strategic assumption, you need to find an indicator that's relevant to it. Our management reports and scorecards have grown cumbersome and contradictory because they list metrics that test unimportant assumptions and metrics that are irrelevant to any assumption. If you want to focus on data that can improve decisions, you must find a way to screen indicators for relevance.

There's still no need to call the bright consultant who took you to lunch or even to turn on your computer. Just pull out a piece of paper and pencil, and start with the definition I set out in the previous chapter: a performance indicator is relevant to a strategic assumption if the assumption's truth or falsity greatly affects the results you expect. The results from an irrelevant indicator are equally likely whether your assumptions are true or false.

Lurking behind this definition, as explained in the final section of this chapter, is a marriage of several aspects of Bayesian probability and information theory. In essence, it picks out tests whose expected results depend on which assumption is true in a set of competing assumptions. Most people managing an office or a business don't have the time to formulate sets of competing assumptions. That's okay; we test them one at a time until we find one that works. The definition works for one-at-a-time tests.

Choose a strategic assumption to test. It should be important in the sense that a mistake about it would have a big impact on what you expect to accomplish. And it should be unsettled, like the assumptions in the eight-line strategies of Chapter Two. Since it's easiest to apply this definition to performance indicators by thinking about favorable and unfavorable results separately, the relevance screen has two parts.

Let's start with results that would be unfavorable to the assumption you're testing. For example, say that you believe a staff training program will increase customer satisfaction with your home electronic and electrical systems business. Would an indicator tracking positive and negative evaluations collected in random follow-up calls to customers be relevant?

The first part of the relevance screen, shown in Figure 4.1, asks whether an indicator's results could possibly disprove your assumption. Clearly it's possible that enough customers would give you negative feedback in your follow-up calls to show something was wrong with the training. Follow-up call responses are relevant in this sense to training effectiveness.

To take another example, suppose one of your systems specialists wants to test satisfaction by offering small discounts to

Figure 4.1 Relevance Screen

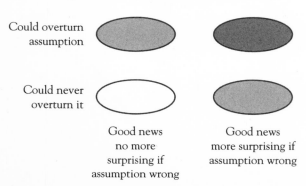

Could overturn assumption

Could never overturn it

Good news
no more
surprising if
assumption wrong

Good news
more surprising if
assumption wrong

customers. The discount would be available to any customer who made a recommendation that resulted in new business. As long as the discounts are small, customer recommendations show enthusiasm. But even a disappointing result from the recommendation discount program wouldn't prove dissatisfaction (or, more accurately, disprove satisfaction). Customers might just be too busy to take the trouble. Customer recommendations are less relevant than follow-up calls to training effectiveness.

Indicators whose results have the potential to disprove an assumption fall in the upper half of a relevance screen like the one shown in Figure 4.1. Indicators whose results just don't have the power to overturn an assumption fall in the bottom half.

The second half of the screen focuses on possible results that would be favorable to an assumption. The Saatchi & Saatchi case shows it's easy to embrace red herrings that look as if they support your theory of your business but are actually irrelevant to it. And it's easy to fall into the confirming evidence trap that Peter Schnall is exorcising from Capital One. So you want to ask whether good news on a performance indicator really supports the assumption it's supposed to test.

The definition basically says that good news can support an assumption if it casts doubt on the idea that the assumption is wrong. To apply it, consider the kinds of results from each indicator you're screening that might seem favorable to your assumption. Ask yourself how surprising such good news would be. Then ask whether it would be a lot more surprising if you somehow knew the assumption was wrong. If the falsity of your assumption makes a favorable result more surprising, it's a relevant indicator.

Even the recommendation discount program could be relevant to your training effectiveness assumption on this dimension of the screen. The best way to structure it would be to start the discount program before the training. It would be very surprising to see recommendations increase after a training program if the program were ineffective.

Indicators whose favorable results would be a lot more surprising if your assumptions were wrong fall on the right side of the relevance screen in Figure 4.1. Indicators whose results are equally likely whether your assumptions are true or false fall on the left side. The indicators that are most relevant to an assumption fall in the top right circle; the least relevant indicators fall in the bottom left circle. The other two circles house indicators that are partially relevant to an assumption. You can think of the screen as separating indicators into three categories of relevance to a strategic assumption: high (upper right), low (lower left), and medium (everywhere else).

The main purpose of this screen is to pick out the handful of indicators most relevant to each key assumption you want to test. But it also checks whether the assumption you're testing really says anything. Go back to the first half of the screen. Suppose none of the indicators in your management report has the power to overturn your assumption. In fact, suppose none of them could yield a result that was even surprising in the light of the assumption. And suppose you can't devise any indicator that might cast doubt on the assumption. In that case, your assumption may not be saying anything.

For example, suppose you sold a unique line of clothing and were trying to understand what drives sales. You might have a list of assumptions about price, distribution, and inventory availability. But suppose you added the assumption that higher demand will increase sales. It seems reasonable because we all know that markets depend on supply and demand. But what if there's no way to measure demand for your clothing line other than by its sales? After all, the line is unique. If there's no independent way to measure demand, the assumption can't do you much good. Although there are plenty of ways you might raise sales, you could never tell whether they were working by raising demand or doing something else. There's no indicator that could falsify the assumption.

The first half of the relevance screen, then, serves as a final check that your assumption means something. It's always possible you won't find an indicator relevant to a valid assumption. But the relevance screen will always alert you if you're inadvertently looking for indicators relevant to an assumption that doesn't say anything.

Screening Indicators for Specificity and Putting the Two Screens Together

Even if you find an indicator that's highly relevant to a key assumption, it may be too vague to be useful. All other things equal, a more specific performance measure will be more valuable than a less specific one. For example, a measure of the hours worked in a three-person car repair shop tells the shop owner more than a record of how many people worked each day. If you want to find the best indicator to test an assumption, you need to screen the alternatives for specificity as well as relevance.

Specificity is about precision. It gets at how many different possible results you could reasonably expect an indicator to yield. Unlike the relevance screen, this is old news. It's very close to the classic definition of information, where the information content of a measure tells you how surprising on average its various results are.

In fact, you might think of specificity as what the information revolution changed. It basically increased the aggregate specificity of all of the information at our disposal. Business applications measure content in the form of message and file sizes all the time. And the search for more specificity is arguably behind the ever-growing length of our management reports. What the information revolution did not affect was relevance.

The mathematical definition of information—and, by extension, specificity—is a bit complicated. But it turns out you can extract the two main ingredients in an intuitive way. The first ingredient is the number of distinct possible results or outcomes you get when you apply a measure. If it usually yields a 1 or a 2 but on rare occasions other numbers up through 99, for instance, you could say it yields one of two typical results. Another measure that yields 1 through 99 with equal likelihood, however, yields nearly a hundred. It's more informative. And if the two measures are equally relevant to some assumption, the latter is more likely to detect a mistake should the assumption be wrong.

Unlike relevance, specificity is independent of what you want to do with an indicator. An indicator's specificity will be the same regardless of the assumption you're testing. This has always been the problem with specificity and the related concept of information: they ignore context. Harnessed alongside a screen for relevance, however, specificity neatly completes the job of ranking a set of performance indicators.

Start by estimating how many different results each indicator you're screening typically yields. Don't worry about very rare outcomes. For example, let's say you're looking at a report that gives monthly late delivery percentages for seven divisions. You could simply count how many different percentage values you see recurring in the monthly numbers for the seven divisions. If most of the percentage values recur, say, three or four times, don't count the outliers that occur just once.

Indicators that yield one of a large number of possible results fall in the upper half of the specificity screen in Figure 4.2. Those that typically yield one of only a small number of possible results fall in the bottom half. How you draw the line between a large and small number of possible results depends on your indicators. You want to divide them up so that fewer than half of the indicators fall in the upper half of the screen.

Figure 4.2 Specificity Screen

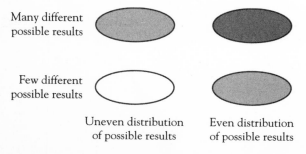

Many different possible results

Few different possible results

Uneven distribution of possible results   Even distribution of possible results

The second ingredient for an indicator's specificity looks at how frequently those possible results recur. If the likelihood or frequency of an indicator's possible results is fairly even, it should fall on the right half of the screen in Figure 4.2. If the likelihood or frequency of those possible results is very uneven, it should fall to the left. Suppose, for example, that one way to measure late deliveries yields 10 percent half the time, 5 percent a quarter of the time, and 15 and 20 percent an eighth of the time each. And say another way to measure late deliveries yields 5 percent, 12 percent, and 20 percent a third of the time each. The second measure has a more even likelihood of different results—which is better for specificity—even though it has fewer recurring different outcomes. This part of the screen ensures that results really tell you something—that the typical measurement of an indicator excludes reasonably probable, and not just remotely unlikely, alternatives.

Like the relevance screen, the specificity screen divides indicators into three categories. High-specificity indicators fall in the upper-right part of the screen, while low-specificity ones fall in the lower left. Medium-specificity indicators fall in between.

Together the two screens tell you all there is to know about the value of an indicator given whatever assumption you need to test. Intuitively we've just screened for relevance and accuracy, which is a little like aim and consistency. But it makes mathematical sense too: the screens are based on the two components of the amount of uncertainty that an indicator can take out of an assumption.[10]

For any strategic assumption you need to test, you now have a high-, medium-, and low-relevance ranking of a set of possible indicators. And you have a high-, medium-, and low-specificity ranking of those indicators. It's a simple matter to put the two screens together for an overall ranking of how well each indicator tests the assumption. You can allocate the indicators to the nine circles of a metrics matrix for each assumption you need to test, like the one pictured in Figure 4.3.

High-specificity indicators fall in the top row and low-specificity indicators in the bottom row of a metrics matrix.

Figure 4.3 Metrics Matrix

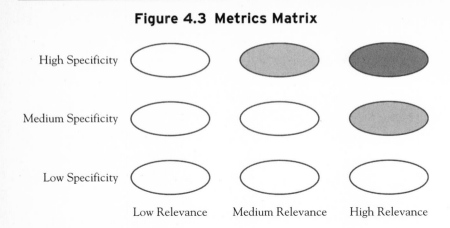

The same indicators will fall in the same rows of matrices for different assumptions because specificity is independent of the assumption they test. High-relevance indicators fall in the right-hand column, and low-relevance ones in the left-hand column. The same indicators naturally fall in different columns of matrices for different assumptions because relevance depends on assumptions.

For any assumption you need to test, the best indicators are in upper right oval, shaded dark gray here. Any of these will be an outstanding indicator or metric for the assumption. If there are no indicators that made it into the upper right oval, check the two closest ovals, shaded light gray. They aren't quite as good, because they reflect a deficiency in one of the components of relevance or one of the components of specificity. But they're still going to be useful.

To see how the screens work, let's use them to rank some alternative indicators for one of the assumptions in Chapter Two's kimono sales example. The strategy assumes that fifteen new customers come into the store each day because of the new line of kimono near the window. Say you might want to evaluate three indicators to see if you're right:

1. The difference between one month's average daily customers before and after introducing kimono to the store

2. Responses over a week from customers at the cash register to the question, "Did you come in because of the kimono?"

3. A half-day survey of all customers leaving the store

Start with the two parts of the relevance screen. Which indicators could overturn your assumption of fifteen new daily customers? The second and third could, but not the first: an unchanged monthly average could always reflect some negative factor off-setting effective kimono. And which indicators' positive results would be more surprising if you were wrong? Good news from the first and third indicators would be surprising if kimono were not really drawing customers. But a favorable result from the second could be misleading: "yeses" could always come from customers who would come in anyway.

To capture these comparisons, identify the three indicators on sticky notes, and attach them to the relevance screen in Figure 4.1: indicator 1 goes in the lower-right circle corresponding to the no and yes answers above; indicator 2 goes in the upper left circle because of the yes and no answers above; and indicator 3 goes in the upper right circle because of the two yeses (as in Figure 4.4).

Move on to the specificity screen. Which indicators could yield more distinct possible results over different time periods? The first could yield several thousand distinct possible averages,

Figure 4.4 Relevance Screen for the Kimono Example

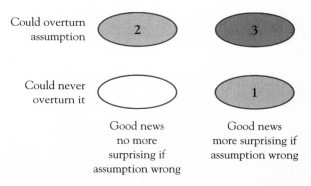

Could overturn
assumption

2   3

Could never
overturn it

1

Good news
no more
surprising if
assumption wrong

Good news
more surprising if
assumption wrong

while the second is limited to the number of purchasing customers in a week—let's say roughly 10 percent, or seventy-five—and
the third is limited to the number of customers in a four-hour
sample—also about seventy-five.[11] And which indicators' results
would you expect to be most evenly distributed? Nothing apart
from the actual effectiveness of kimono biases the possible results
of the first and third indicators toward any particular values. But
we already saw that low values were less likely for the second.

Pull out three more sticky notes. Place indicator 1 in the upper-
right circle because of the two yeses, indicator 2 in the lower-left
because of the two noes, and indicator 3 in the lower-right circle because of the no and yes answers (Figure 4.5).

The shading of the screens helps you put their results together.
For example, indicator 1 has medium relevance and high specificity for the assumption about new store traffic due to the kimono, so
it belongs in the middle top circle of a metrics matrix. The second
indicator belongs in the middle bottom circle of the matrix because
it has medium relevance and low specificity. And the third response
belongs in the right middle circle because it has high relevance and
medium specificity.

The result is a tie between the first indicator, which compares
monthly averages, and the third indicator, which requires you to
pay someone to survey customers for four hours (Figure 4.6). Either
one will provide an acceptable, if not great, test of the assumption that kimono are driving a 10 percent increase in store traffic.

Figure 4.5 Specificity Screen for the Kimono Example

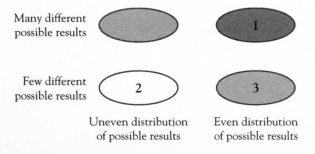

Many different
possible results

Few different
possible results

Uneven distribution
of possible results

Even distribution
of possible results

Figure 4.6 Metrics Matrix for the Kimono Example

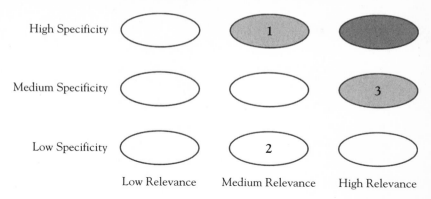

If you do not need to test your strategy immediately, you can save yourself the cost of the survey.

As an example of how to put a metrics matrix to work, suppose you want to construct a dashboard for your division over the next month. You despair of doing this because your division's monthly management report is forty pages long. The joke in the office is that the appendix starts after the title. But you have filled out an eight-line strategy of key unsettled issues for the month. This is the time to pull it out.

For each of the assumptions on your eight-line strategy—let's say you thought them up after last month's performance review—rank the most promising metrics in your management report. Look for the best performer in each of the eight metrics matrices you construct. The resulting metrics are your dashboard. The power of the metrics matrix is that you've made a highly discriminating selection of key performance indicators without even pulling out a calculator.

The Metrics Matrix and the Search for Better Indicators

In fact, the method is so discriminating that there may be no metrics in any of the three top right ovals of the metrics matrix for one of your key assumptions. Every time this happens—every time you find you can't test an assumption that's important and unsettled—you've identified a question you won't be able to answer when the next results come in. If you miss a target that seems reasonable given your assumptions but you lack an indicator for one of those assumptions, you won't know whether your plan is wrong or whether you didn't marshal all the resources and effort you needed.

Imagine that sales of a cereal brand you manage are slipping. You suspect customers are becoming price conscious and would prefer a 5 percent price reduction with dried apple in place of the exotic dried star fruit you've been selling. The only way to find out is try it out. You track the cereal's sales and store prices to get a quick read on the basis of one month's results. But at the end of the month, you realize your store inventory model isn't very precise, so you can't tell how much of what sold had dried apple in place of star fruit. You've lost a month for turning around the decline.

Just about everyone who runs an office or a division or a company has had the experience of missing a goal and not being sure what went wrong. What's new here is that the metrics matrix gives you advance warning of the kind of indicator that can answer your questions. The metrics matrix can't help you see into the future, but it can help you see what you may need in the future. And that lets you do something about it.

In the case of the cereal brand manager, there is a crystal-clear assumption: a cereal that substitutes apples for star fruit and is 5 percent cheaper will sell better. There is also an indicator in the form of monthly sales (plus actual prices) that looks like it might test it. By itself, however, a monthly sales indicator turns out to be irrelevant to the assumption. And the reason that it's irrelevant is the key to devising a better set of indicators for the brand manager's experiment.

Monthly sales are irrelevant to the apple-and-lower-price idea because an encouraging result is almost as likely if the idea is wrong. Since you don't know how much new inventory is on store shelves, strong sales could reflect a surge in appetite for the old product that stores could still satisfy. Worse still, a poor monthly sales result can't challenge the apple-and-lower-price idea by itself. Once again inventory is the culprit: the poor result could reflect lots of old inventory on store shelves together with a collapse in customers' appetite for star fruit. An indicator for monthly sales, unsupported by other measures, fails both prongs of the relevance test for your new product idea.

To test the new strategy, you need a measure of store inventory as well as monthly sales and store prices. Then you'll know whether the sales results you measure really reflect a response to the new product and the new prices.

You might have caught the oversight by recognizing you were really making two assumptions. First, you thought you could hit a particular sales target by switching to dried apples and lowering prices. Second, you thought your distribution channel could make the switch to dried apples in time to test the concept.

Even if you didn't split out the two assumptions, though, the relevance test in this chapter would have warned you that you needed another performance metric. Moreover, it would have helped you see just what that metric needed to measure. Here are three rules of thumb for devising new indicators to see if your ideas are working. I'll illustrate them with new assumptions from three lines of business you might want to test.

- *Rule 1: Effects. Imagine what effects you would see if your assumption were right.*

For example, say you want to test the assumption that customers of your hot drinks chain value never having to wait too long but don't care for the drab sameness of your stores. You might try to increase market share by opening stores with a radically different look that advertised their reliable order processing.

Or suppose you assumed customers of your airline would pay for extra legroom even though we're a bunch of bargain-hunting scrooges when it comes to every other aspect of airline travel. The acid test would be whether we opted for seats with more legroom once we had selected a flight on the basis of schedule and destination.

As a final example, you might assume you could increase the number of usable new ideas your lab produced without increasing costs by following a fast-to-fail rule. You could try setting early goals for new projects to nip the unpromising ones in the bud.

- *Rule 2: Measurability. Look for ways to measure those effects.*

In the case of the hot drinks chain, you could measure the number of customers who come to a location with a new look from older ones that resemble one another. One way might be to have the older stores give away discount tickets on future drinks at any store, including one with a new look, in the chain. Then you could count the number of tickets redeemed at the newer locations. Of course, you would also have to keep tabs on the waiting time at the new locations.

The airline could create a class that differed from coach only in the legroom afforded by its seats. Ideally you would try it out on airplanes that had better-spaced rows scattered throughout the cabin. But that's impractical. At the very least, though, you would need to make explicit offers to your flyers that emphasized same service, just more legroom. Then you could experiment with pricing to see what people would pay.

The lab director would probably want to measure how many projects his teams terminated under the new fast-to-fail rule. Let's assume the lab also collects data for its return on investment. The new measure would show whether more project terminations increased the productivity of each dollar spent on research.

- *Rule 3: Unlikelihood. Make sure what you measure would be unlikely if your assumption were wrong.*

This last consideration would have ruled out a simple measure of sales at the hot drinks chain locations with a new look. Good news might just mean people are looking for a change or you found some underserved neighborhoods. By tracking customers from older locations, though, you can tell whether the new locations attract more customers from old stores than the typical old store does. That's what you would expect if your customers were really looking for interesting decor with reliable waiting times. It would be surprising to find a disproportionate number of old customers at new locations that shared only waiting times with their older sister stores for any other reason.

By the same token, just offering flyers a better class of coach that includes more legroom wouldn't tell you how much your customers really value legroom. Good results from the new class of service could reflect customers hoping to eat or sleep better who don't care about legroom. But if a lot of customers take up a service offer that's explicitly the same as coach except for legroom, there's only one explanation.

Just measuring new project terminations in the research lab won't test your fast-to-fail rule either. A lot of project terminations could well raise return on investment in research simply by reducing that investment. What you want to test is whether project terminations can improve results by increasing the number of usable ideas. You need an extra measure for the number of project launches. It would really be surprising if more projects stopped, more new ones started, and results improved for any reason other than that your fast-to-fail rule released resources for more new projects. In essence, you need to make an extra assumption about how fast-to-fail works in the lab.

Assumptions about risks pose a tricky problem for devising new metrics. It might seem you need to measure the whole distribution of possible outcomes of whatever risk factor keeps you from reliably hitting your goals. All you need to do, however, is measure the actual value of that risk factor over a given performance period to compare with your planning assumption for the factor over that period. If you think oil prices will affect your business results next month, for example, you need to state the assumed price on which you're basing your goals and then measure the actual average for the month.

If the factor is highly uncertain, of course, the actual value over a performance period will probably diverge from your planning assumption. But the real reason to measure the value of a risk factor isn't just to check how well you can forecast the unknown. By measuring the actual values of a risk factor, you can test whether you're right about how the factor affects your results.

As for remembering these three rules to devise metrics for untested assumptions, the obvious acronym, emu (effects, measurability, unlikelihood), fails my own relevance test: I can't for the life of me find a link between the rules and emus. There are too many acronyms in business books anyway. So try not to think of small birds that stick their heads in the sand when you want to recall what to do about a critical assumption untested by any of your current metrics.

Strategy Metrics, Managerial Fallibilism, and the End of Magical Thinking

Pause for a moment to look back at what this method for choosing metrics lets you do. Without a single calculation, it helps you make a highly discriminating evaluation of potentially large numbers of indicators, and it focuses that evaluation on how you're actually trying to solve whatever problems you face. This is the kind of evaluation we usually have to throw over the wall to the statisticians in the hope that whatever bubbles back up to the surface of their mote is at least recognizable. So the question is why such a simple way to choose indicators could possibly work.

The metrics matrix combines parts of Bayesian probability and information theory in an intuitive tool. It works because the strengths of these two increasingly important management disciplines patch one another's gaps if you choose the parts carefully.

The idea behind Bayes' theorem is simple: new evidence can help you decide which of several competing assumptions to believe when you're trying to understand how something works. Software engineers use it in word processing and e-mail features that try to guess the word or name you've started to type. Some people say the theorem shows how evidence confirms assumptions. But its real strength is keeping track of how many competing assumptions a new piece of evidence rules out or makes doubtful.[12]

Bayesian probability is fairly good at identifying relevant data. It says a piece of evidence should change your mind if it's a lot more likely under some assumptions than others. Doctors and epidemiologists use this idea in the form of type I and type II errors. Type I errors are false positives such as testing positive for bird flu when you're actually healthy. Type II errors are false negatives such as thinking you're clear of poison ivy after a walk when in fact you're about to break out in a rash.

The question in the relevance screen about the ability of an indicator to overturn your assumption avoids type I errors. Indicator results that would be very surprising if your assumption were true make false positives unlikely. The question whether some results would be surprising if your assumption were wrong avoids type II errors. Such results make false negatives unlikely since you need your assumption to explain them.

Bayesian probability also reflects the specificity of new evidence. But it does so in a way that can be misleading. The theorem makes it appear that new evidence can prove even universal assumptions when in fact it's only ruling out some of the alternatives. You might say that Bayesian probability approaches learning by measuring what we know. This is dangerous because of the enormous appeal of red herrings that look as if they support our pet theories when they actually do not.

Fortunately, information theory provides a framework that recognizes the persistence of uncertainty about universal assumptions even in the face of good evidence. It never teases you away from fallibilism.

Information theory is the field of twentieth-century mathematics that helps telephone companies determine how much line capacity they need. It also drives the algorithms that pack music into CDs and MP3 files. It focuses on how much detail you need to recognize a message. My agent, Howard Yoon, gives a classic example: "Only infrmtn esentl to undrstandg mst b transmtd." Maybe he was really giving me a subliminal message to keep this book short. But it's a great illustration of the theory's focus on what's unnecessary for reducing uncertainty about your assumptions—whether you're talking about the vowels in a text message or irrelevant and redundant indicators in a performance report. It's a theory about what doesn't matter.

Information theory approaches learning by measuring what we don't know. When it looks at a result from an indicator, for example, it asks how many other results you might have obtained. This leads to a clear notion of specificity or information content called entropy.[13] So far, however, the theory's treatment of relevance is, to use a less technical term, clunky.

Framing Bayesian probability in terms of information theory's measures of what we don't know gives clear interpretations of both relevance and specificity. The questions in the relevance and specificity screens reflect those interpretations. Readers who want to write computer routines to automate the screens can take a look at how I'm formulating relevance in the endnotes.[14] But what's important for the argument of the book is the fact that a rigorous framework backs up the interpretations. It's important for what it says about relevance as well as the relationship of relevance and specificity.

First, the framework defines relevance with respect to assumptions, so it lends weight to the idea that relevance depends not on our problems but on the assumptions we make to solve them. This is why the value of a given piece of information to people solving the same problem in different ways will vary.

Second, the framework construes relevance and specificity as two parts of the larger concept of mutual information. Information theorists define mutual information as the amount of information that something like an indicator provides about something like a set of competing assumptions. The concept is central to gene sequencing. Elegantly, it's the simple sum of relevance, as I've defined it, and specificity. That's why you can put the screens for the relevance and specificity of an indicator together and read off the indicator's value given your assumptions. The screens let you price information.

The metrics matrix seems to provide a principled way to pare down balanced scorecards that have grown fat. That's no small thing since thousands of executives in Europe, the United States, and Japan are looking to do just that. But I think it provides something more important: it puts assumptions at the heart of fact-based decisions about our businesses, agencies, and organizations—and not just any assumptions.

The metrics matrix forces you to make assumptions that really say something. Remember what happens if you look for indicators to test an assumption that's so weak it can't rule out any course of action. All of your indicators will fail the relevance test. Nothing can be relevant—in the sense of this book—to something that's true no matter how your business actually works or how your environment is changing.

So while the metrics matrix seems to focus on your choice of performance indicators, it blows back on the assumptions you're using to give direction to your office or organization. It forces you to make assumptions about how to achieve your goals.

Those assumptions can't just be lists of requirements for achieving your goals, like the list of ingredients for a soufflé. Assumptions that assert the requirements of a goal are necessarily true if the goal is achieved. Remember that while they can signal when you're off the mark, they say little about how to achieve them. The metrics matrix demands assumptions that prescribe ways to get things done, as does the recipe for a soufflé. They may be wrong. Your indicators will help you tell.

For all their advantages, balanced scorecards rarely test strategies. As we've seen, people tend to use them to test requirements for success instead. I suppose that's more of a problem with how we use balanced scorecards than with the scorecards themselves. But I think they're too permissive. They invite us to list requirements for success—like the processes we must manage to approach our customer goals—and think it's a strategy.

Suppose your goal is to launch a new model of jumbo aircraft meeting stringent customer needs for performance and on-time delivery. Even the best scorecard systems will tempt you to work backward and specify requirements for the hundreds of major research, procurement, logistics, manufacturing, assembly, testing, and marketing processes needed to meet the goal. But they're just requirements. They're like the eggs, flour, milk, and soufflé dish needed for a soufflé. You could meet them all and still find yourself two years late in delivering the new jet.

Simple as it, a metrics matrix for the project would have kicked up a problem with your list of process requirements. Once you've settled on an indicator for project completion, you'll have a problem with indicators to test your assumptions about the processes it requires. By definition, there will never be a situation where you could meet your project goal and miss a process requirement. The process indicators will fail the relevance screen since, again by definition, no result could overturn the assumption it tests in any scenario where you've managed to deliver a good plane on time.

What the matrix shows is that such requirements tell you nothing beyond what you know if you've succeeded in the project. Like the list of ingredients of a soufflé, they don't tell you how to succeed. You need other kinds of assumptions to do that. For example, you might assume that the best way to cope with the complexity of a massive contemporary aircraft electronic entertainment system is to subcontract the work to the Japanese firms that have handled avionics for U.S. fighters since the 1970s. The assumption may be wrong, but it tells you what to do. It's the beginning of a strategy you can test and improve. You'll need more assumptions like it.

The problem is that we rarely mistake requirements but often pursue the wrong strategy. By testing something that is rarely wrong, balanced scorecards can lead to a dangerous sense of infallibility. That may be an even bigger problem with how we use them than their tendency to grow endlessly.

The treatment in the next chapter of performance reviews—and their transformation into what I call strategy reviews—discusses the damage that supposedly infallible strategies can do to enterprise morale. One of their consequences is to turn every performance gap into an execution problem, as if there were no such thing as a planning or strategic error. What's ironic is that few supporters of managerial infallibility really mean to support it. We back into it through requirements-based planning and the scorecards that let us get away with it.

For now, it's enough to note the strange similarity between plans based solely on requirements and Homeric myths. After all, once you've set a final goal, there's some certainty about what it requires. You can derive requirements from a goal. If the goal is to get to the church on time, you must leave home before the wedding hour. What you don't get from a list of requirements is anything speculative. A route to get to the church in under an hour might be useful, for instance, but it will never drop out of a list of requirements. That route is a theory. It may even be wrong.

We crave requirements because we want to be right. We seek in our plans a certitude that has evaporated since the disappearance of the gods whose whisperings in the ears of the Homeric heroes explained all the chances and vagaries of war. The hope for certainty about anything as complex as business and government is a holdover from our heritage of magical thinking. And so we mistake requirements for strategies. The irony is that we have no real need of certainty or magical thinking. We need only be bold in the face of unavoidable error and quick to learn by recognizing it.

5

THREE KINDS OF PERFORMANCE GAPS AND THE STRATEGY REVIEW

The three sorts of knowledge form a tripod:
if any leg were lost, no part would stand.
—*Donald Davidson*

In the winter of 2000–2001, Cisco had a near-death experience. It missed the downturn in the economy. It fired eighty-five hundred employees—about a fifth of its staff—and wrote off $2.2 billion of fast-obsolescing unsold inventory. Cisco stock was down 83 percent by April 2001. The reason was a mistaken growth assumption.

By 2000, Cisco had enjoyed ten years of quarterly growth. Internet router components being in short supply, that growth record seemed to justify aggressive anticipatory component procurement.[1] But dot-com companies were failing and reselling scarcely used Cisco equipment. And while suppliers like Solectron and Xilinx saw signs of a slowdown in the summer of 2000, Cisco didn't react until it missed its sales projections in the middle of December.[2]

The technology media were already eager to take Cisco down a peg after the news frenzy sparked by its announcement that it could close its monthly books within a day. Cisco's Internet-based ledger system certainly was impressive. But in fairness, only the news media ever thought the system could make up for poor judgment. When journalists pounced on him after the April 2001 crackup, CFO Larry Carter said sarcastically, "We're developing a new module for our system right now. It's called a crystal ball."[3]

Bill Bien, a director of strategic planning at Cisco, is getting ready to leave for Saudi Arabia when I call to ask how the crystal ball has worked out. As he ticks off the firm's five clusters of performance indicators—growth, profitability, market share, customer satisfaction, and product quality—he discovers that the Saudi visa form asks him to agree to be executed if he breaks any major laws of the Kingdom.[4] This puts a damper on my question about the relative importance of strategy and execution.

Bill reminds me of his counterpart at Toyota, insisting that good planning is more art than science. Even so, there's plenty of science in the crystal-clear handful of indicators he's described for a company threatened by inventory pileups and stock-outs. None of those indicators pretends to see into the future of growth. But they systematically test possible assumptions about growth for mistakes.

Suppose sales growth looks reassuringly high. Might it be spurious, a result of inadvertently underpricing the product? The indicators for profitability and market share will show if Cisco is merely growing at the expense of competitors. That's not a bad thing, but it undermines the assumption that total demand is growing.

Suppose that sales growth seems alarmingly weak. Might that also be a false signal? The indicators for customer satisfaction and product quality will show whether Cisco is losing sales to higher-quality competition. That in itself is important to know, but it also means that underlying demand may not be slowing.

Cisco's next difficult battle may have nothing to do with inventory and the correct interpretation of growth indicators. It has nevertheless designed a short, elegant list of upstream and downstream indicators to test a wide range of assumptions about demand. Although the list includes several indicators reflecting upstream controllable success factors like quality and satisfaction, it also focuses on the accuracy of downstream planning assumptions about the growth and profitability it hopes to achieve. Here's a firm that has learned to use performance indicators to test strategy as well as manage execution.

This chapter and the next argue that unless organizations radically change how they use performance results, their expanding information resources will paralyze them. Performance results may still assess the execution of strategic plans—their traditional focus—but should do so only as a by-product of testing strategic assumptions.

You might think you can check up on the quality of execution without throwing your basic strategic assumptions into question. But you'll find yourself generating a potentially limitless list of performance requirements if you try. There's no way to know what aspects of execution matter without making assumptions about how your business works. And there is no way to know whether those assumptions are right without testing them. Even if you care only about execution, I argue, you must use performance results to test strategic assumptions at some level of generality.

A big reason we think we can review execution without reviewing strategy is that we confuse execution with tactics or operations. Tactics are a way of implementing a strategy, according to the first section of this chapter, just as strategy is a way of achieving a goal. Strategy may be irrelevant to someone responsible only for tactics. And if you think of execution as tactics, strategy may be irrelevant to it too.

Execution, however, applies to a broader sense of strategy: the assumptions we make about what tactics will achieve any given goal. Execution distinguishes what we do from what we intend to do about those tactics, so it's intimately bound up with strategy in the sense of the assumptions you make about how to succeed. That's why progressive managers assess strategy as well as execution even in organizational functions far removed from enterprise-wide strategic planning.

The first section of this chapter uses these distinctions to define three kinds of performance gaps based on the three kinds of assumptions you might make to meet a goal. Some of your assumptions refer to actions you think you can take, some refer to risks, and some relate your actions and risks to your goals. All of them may be wrong. So the first section splits any difference between actual and expected performance results into an execution gap, an uncontrollable gap, and a strategy gap.

The second section proposes a model strategy review that explicitly challenges strategic plans and assumptions in place of traditional reviews of performance results that focus only on the quality of execution. Strategy reviews look at every performance period as a controlled experiment. These experiments naturally test work effort and risk forecasts. But they also test the quality of the plans or assumptions relating that effort and those forecasts to results. Strategy reviews highlight and track the execution, uncontrollable, and strategy gaps underlying the performance results of each part of your organization.

The third section looks into what you can do about strategy gaps. It proposes profit redenomination, or the redefinition of what aspect of your operations you are trying to make profitable, as a way of dealing with persistent strategy errors. It also clarifies what performance gaps can tell you about the individual assumptions your metrics test. It's true that you can't always be sure which assumption is responsible for a bad result. Assumptions operate together as a network to yield expectations much as the parts of a scientific theory or the definitions of foreign words work together to help us interpret lab results or unfamiliar languages. But the section shows this won't keep you from using performance results to test individual assumptions as a practical matter.

The last section argues that the biggest benefit of strategy reviews is motivational. Organizations that don't look for strategy errors in their performance results force their operating managers to protect themselves from being blamed for missing unrealistic goals, and that usually means sandbagging performance projections.

But experience becomes useless if you set goals and expectations based on what's safe given your current understanding of your business. Organizations that pin performance gaps wholly on execution end up transforming the narrow risk of admitting planning errors into a wider risk of deteriorating execution and stalled growth.

Triangular Definitions

To learn from your performance results, you need to relate them to the assumptions you've made in setting your goals. This is true even if you're trying only to make better and fairer assessments of execution efforts against your plans. To judge those efforts fairly, you have to know whether your goals were fair and the assumptions behind them valid. So this section breaks the differences between your goals and what you actually achieve into three parts: strategy gaps, uncontrollable gaps, and execution gaps. Strategy and execution gaps basically separate the impact of flaws in strategic assumptions and performance efforts, and uncontrollable gaps pick up the impact of known risks. It's a step beyond current best practice in performance management and strategic planning, but a number of companies in addition to Cisco are heading in this direction.[5]

Strategy gaps reflect the difference between the goal you set and the goal you should have set. They check the quality of your planning assumptions. They're not about better forecasts—plenty of risk factors are simply unpredictable—but about better theories of your business. A zero gap means a goal was fair.

Uncontrollable gaps reflect the difference between the goal you should have set given your assumptions about the risk factors you've identified and the result you and your team should have achieved given the way those risks turned out. Say you set performance goals based on a perfect model for your division, and execution is flawless. Then a gap between your goals and actual results can arise only from errors in your forecast for the risk factors in the model. That's the uncontrollable gap.

Execution gaps reflect the difference between what you and your team should have achieved given the way the risk factors you've identified turned out and your actual final result. These gaps are what are left when you subtract strategy and uncontrollable gaps from any difference between goals and actual results. Figure 5.1 illustrates the decomposition of a performance surprise into the three kinds of gaps.

Figure 5.1 Types of Performance Gaps

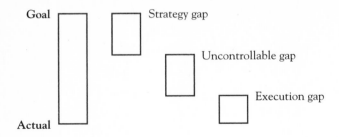

Execution gaps work a little like same-store results for a retail chain. Same-store profits reveal whether a chain is getting more productive. Overall profits are misleading because the chain could have opened a raft of new locations with lower initial efficiency. Same-store sales correct for differences due to the new locations.

Even same-store results can reflect all three types of gaps, however. For example, a fall-off in McDonald's U.S. same-store performance between 2000 and 2002 signaled an unaccommodated shift toward lighter American diets (strategy) as well as recession (uncontrollable) and operating problems (execution) in the home market. In cases like this, a systematic review of all three gaps can isolate what's really due to execution.

Let's take a close look at a simple example. Imagine you expected an assistant to review ten loan applications today, but he gets through only six, so the overall performance shortfall is four. You thought a recent change in the application process would have little impact on the complexity of the loan files, but you weren't sure, so you kept track of file lengths—in other words, you tested your assumption. It turns out that the new files are about 25 percent longer than the old ones. As a first estimate, you decide you should have expected your assistant to get through just eight of the new applications instead of ten—a strategy gap of two. You also find that a computer crash kept your assistant from finishing another file—an uncontrollable gap of one. So you conclude it would have been fair to hold your assistant accountable for review-ing seven files instead of six, an execution gap of one.

In this example, you tracked three assumptions: the number of files your assistant reviewed in a day, whether the computer system would be up for a full day's work, and whether new files are harder to review than previous ones. Variations of these assump-tions lead to the same picture of performance. For example, you might have tracked how many files your assistant completed in an hour of supervised work (let's say one instead of one and a quarter in the days when files were simpler), how many hours the computer system was available (seven), and how many files your assistant completed (six). In the latter case, the first assumption reveals a strategy gap of two files since it's no longer realistic to expect anyone to get through ten files in eight hours. The second assumption reveals an uncontrollable gap of one file correspond-ing to the hour of downtime. And the third assumption reveals an execution gap of one file, which could reflect an hour of distrac-tions through the day.

What's unusual about both cases is that you separated the impact of poor execution from the effect of an uncontrollable risk factor and a planning error. Most managers find it difficult to isolate the impact of execution problems on messy real-world results with any confidence. The difference is that this approach to planning and performance assessment requires assumptions about what level of execution ensures success. The initial reason for focusing on such testable strategies may have been to expose their weaknesses as quickly as possible. But an immediate side benefit is to let you split the impact of execution and strategy on performance.

One implication of these definitions is that an execution gap for you will generally correspond to a strategy gap for someone else. This is really no different from the familiar phenomenon of cascading goals that FedEx and others formalized in the 1990s, where the output target of one team becomes an input assump-tion for another. In the example here, the execution gap of one file corresponds to a strategy gap for your assistant. Suppose he defines his goal as processing fifteen pages of files per hour (where the length of a typical file is rising, let's say, from twelve to fifteen pages). He might then make a range of assumptions about how to achieve that goal, such as the availability of fact-checking resources, time spent surfing the Internet, caffeine ingested, and so forth. His strategy gap reflects how well he has determined what helps him fix his attention for hours at a time. Your corresponding execution gap reflects whether he's right.

A more realistic example may make it clearer how strategy and execution gaps handle cascading goals where one person's operational or input expectation is another person's final goal. Suppose you're the general manager of an airframe manufacturing division. You assume the division can meet its profit goal for the month by delivering forty general aviation airframes. The profit goal implies your procurement officer can meet the budget's cost estimates for the amount of graphite-polyimide composite resin those airframes require, so you make that assumption explicit as well. You can think of the cost target as a final goal for your procurement chief, but it's also an upstream goal for you. If you end up with an execution gap because the cost estimate is wrong, your procurement chief will have a corresponding strategy gap.

In fact, two people at different levels of an organization should share an assumption, goal, and performance metric wherever the output of one is a critical input for another. What's less clear is why some companies ask all executives to track the exact same set of performance metrics. As long as different kinds of assumptions govern the various responsibilities that executives bear, they will need different metrics to test them. This is true even if everyone measures financial quantities like economic profit the same way to ensure comparability.[6]

What the problem solvers in an organization nevertheless share is the need to test some aspect of strategy. To go back to the airframe example, the general manager is not the only one making assumptions about how to hit a goal. The procurement officer needs to make assumptions about how to deliver materials at the anticipated cost. It's true that the procurement officer's assumptions may be more tactical than the general manager's assumptions, but both are making assumptions about how to achieve aspects of strategy understood broadly as the combination of tactics expected to secure success.

It's no accident that measuring results against two goals—a profit goal and procurement goal in the case of the airframe division's general manager—lets you separate two reasons for a performance shortfall. For example, an execution gap arises if you miss the procurement target. A strategy gap arises if you hit the procurement target but miss the profit target. And several other combinations are possible.

Moreover, you could never separate the effects of planning and execution errors on your results if you measured just downstream indicators like division profit. We tend to think of upstream or operational indicators only as controls or tools for ensuring high-quality execution. Thus you might check the results of a procurement department on which you depend to make sure costs are contained. But that's not strictly necessary: as long as procurement tracks its own results, someone is in a position to address procurement problems. What the general manager could never do without tracking key upstream indicators is determine whether the division's plans were valid.

Nor could you separate the effects of controllable and uncontrollable surprises on your results without measuring risk factors. Many oil companies now split performance surprises into two parts: one reflecting the impact of oil prices and the other reflecting controllable factors.[7] That keeps production units from losing their bonuses just because of a fall in oil prices and distribution units from losing theirs just because of a rise. Without separating uncontrollable and execution gaps, you can't tell which part of an organization is actually improving productivity.

The larger idea is that we need to separate all three kinds of gaps for an objective view of performance. You might say that performance improvement requires a process of triangulation. You can't be sure of the size of an execution gap unless you understand the impact of uncontrollable risk factors—that is, unless you know the size of the uncontrollable gap. You can't be sure of the size of an uncontrollable gap, furthermore, unless you understand whether your goals made sense given your risk assumptions—that is, unless you know the size of the strategy gap. And you can't be sure of the size of a strategy gap unless you know whether execution met your operating assumptions—that is, unless you know the size of the execution gap. They're three legs of the same stool.

This is a strong claim. It means all three gaps are necessary to tell what matters and learn from experience as effectively as possible. You might think triangulation represents just a marginal improvement over performance systems that split performance gaps two ways between controllable and uncontrollable factors. But the failure to recognize strategy gaps as well as execution and uncontrollable gaps could explain why our explanations of performance shortfalls are chronically incomplete—which is what sends us chasing endlessly after more operating data. And it turns out there's a reason to believe that all three gaps are a fundamental part of any collective learning effort.

Donald Davidson, an American philosopher who built the pragmatic approach of his one-time teacher W.V.O. Quine into a compelling and embracing picture of how the mind works and relates to the world, argued that three kinds of knowledge are necessary to learn a language. For him, this was fundamental since he took language to be a template for collective learning. He said our sense of a speaker's beliefs requires some knowledge of the world we share with that speaker, our knowledge of the world naturally depends on our own thoughts about it, and our sense of having thoughts about an independent world—thoughts that might be wrong—depends on experience of others' erroneous beliefs.[8] These three kinds of knowledge—of our self, of others, and of the world—are mutually dependent and mutually irreducible. We don't really start with one and move on to the others.

It's surprising that the three kinds of gaps needed to pinpoint collective performance errors correspond to the three kinds of knowledge needed to pinpoint errors in interpreting a language. But execution gaps really are like surprises about others' beliefs, uncontrollable gaps really are like surprises about the world we share with a speaker, and strategy gaps really are like surprises about the implications of our own beliefs. If three kinds of errors are fundamental to communication, it's not such a stretch to think that three kinds of errors are fundamental to cooperative learning and organizational performance.

The rest of this chapter argues that strategy gaps are more than something that would be nice to add to a planning and performance system. They're a critical part of any collective effort to learn from experience, including performance experience. To the extent we already learn from results, we must be keeping something like strategy gaps in the back of our minds. But we will be much more effective if we make them an explicit part of our plans and performance reviews.

Performance Reviews as Strategy Reviews

This section proposes a model strategy review that explicitly challenges strategic plans and assumptions. It's intended to take the place of traditional monthly and quarterly reviews of performance results that focus on the quality of execution. Strategy reviews look at every performance period as a controlled experiment. These experiments naturally test work effort and risk forecasts, but they also test the quality of the plans or assumptions relating that effort and those forecasts to results.

Strategy reviews resolve surprises from these performance tests into three parts: execution gaps reflecting surprises in work effort, uncontrollable gaps reflecting surprises in risk factors, and strategy gaps reflecting errors in goal setting and your working model of the business. Strategy reviews are possible because of what precedes them: a short list of testable assumptions such as an eight-line strategy and an equally short list of indicators relevant to those assumptions like those screened by a metrics matrix.

You can get an idea of the essence of the shift from performance reviews to strategy reviews from the distance between the following two questions. A lot of the challenges in a traditional monthly or quarterly review of disappointing performance results are really a way of asking: "How are we going to make up this shortfall?" The focus of a strategy review is bracingly different. The operative question is: "Missing a goal is of little use unless you learn something from it, so what do you think we should try doing differently and why?"

By now, you can guess what's going to be required. Don't bother looking for a computer program to download or a consultant to call. The beauty of this system is that it's do-it-yourself. Just make sure you've got a pencil and a piece of paper on hand, gather your team, and then try out these three steps.

Step 1: Evaluate Your Assumptions

This is the straightforward payoff for the work you've already done formulating a short list of key unsettled assumptions and selecting an indicator relevant to each. That work puts you in a position to compare the goal or expectation you've set corresponding to each assumption with the actual result of the indicator you've chosen to test it over any monthly or quarterly performance period.

The relevance and specificity screens for your indicators already guarantee that their results will shed light on your assumptions. In some cases, you'll simply be able to compare a goal backed by one of your assumptions with a result from the corresponding indicator. In others, indicator results will overturn an assumption because they'd be so surprising if it were right—or support it because they'd be so surprising if it were wrong.

As an example of the last two cases—which require inferences about assumptions from results—suppose you assumed that a temporary increase in security measures could help stabilize a town in one of the southern provinces of Afghanistan. Without setting any specific economic goal for this assumption, you might have selected statistics about job seekers as an indicator. It's relevant because a big increase in job seekers would be surprising if the temporary security measures had no ultimate effect: it would support the assumption. If no more people applied for jobs under the security measures than before them, however, the lack of confidence in the measures that you could infer from flat job seeker statistics would undermine the assumption.

These comparisons of results and expectations should be enough to convince you to throw out some of your assumptions. That's no waste; you'll have learned something valuable that competitors afraid of putting their assumptions to a test won't know.

There may also be cases where you prove an assumption. These are more problematic. Any assumptions that you conclusively prove must be fairly weak. For example, you might prove that 10 percent of the people who entered your grocery store last month would buy promotional bottles of two-dollar red wine. But you could never prove the far more useful universal claim that, say, 5 percent of your customers will always buy a two-dollar bottle regardless of the duration of the promotion or their prior experience with the wine.

Although you'll never conclusively prove your more powerful universal assumptions, you'll come to feel that you've settled some of them. Proven or not, these are the assumptions that stand the test of time. They should no longer take up a spot on your short list of key uncertainties. Just make sure your colleagues understand them as part of your organization's hard-won background knowledge before you scratch them off the list.

There's no substitute for judgment in determining when your interim results have settled an assumption, but that's not what's hard about deciding which assumptions need more testing. The hard part is overcoming our natural tendency to focus on the biggest determinants of results regardless of whether we have questions about them.

The tendency may be natural, but it's a mistake because these big determinants crowd out the factors that pose the biggest threats to our plans and contribute the most volatility to our results. For example, think how natural it is to focus on the cost of administrative functions even if they haven't changed in ten years. And yet we routinely ignore tacit assumptions about what our customers really value even though a competitor could find out and take them away from us, with a calamitous effect on our business.

Left on the list are the assumptions that remain unsettled either because we need more information about them or because they're hard to predict. We'll need to test them further—in effect, refresh our forecasts for them—despite that unpredictability. Over time, we'll either learn to forecast their implications better or, like sand in an oyster shell, they'll irritate us and motivate us to devise better ones that are less uncertain.

Step 2: Estimate Your Strategy, Uncontrollable, and Execution Gaps

By now you've compared actual indicator outcomes with the goals or projections corresponding to each of your key assumptions for your last monthly or quarterly performance period. What larger lessons can you draw from this review?

The assumption-driven approach you've been following lets you diagnose the difference between your final goal and final results for the period better than a traditional review of performance results. What's new is that you've set up expectations for each source of uncertainty in your results—those are the goals or projections corresponding to each of your key unsettled assumptions—and found a way to test those expectations with unambiguous metrics screened for relevance.

Start by taking the difference between your final goal and actual final result, which reflects the amount by which you overshot or missed a performance target. To understand fully what caused the difference, you need to split it into three parts: a strategy gap, an uncontrollable gap, and an execution gap. You'll usually want to start with the execution gap (although it makes little difference with simple examples).

To estimate your execution gap, determine what you and your team should have accomplished given the way the risk factors you've identified turned out. Start by checking how your actual final result relates to the actual results for the rest of your indicators. In particular, you want to see whether the relationship you assumed between your final goal and the rest of your projections was right. For example, and oversimplifying a bit, should you have added inputs rather than multiplying them?

Plug your projections for indicators that test inputs like the quality and intensity of work effort or execution into the actual relationship you've discerned among all the indicators. You should substitute your projection for the actual outcome of every indicator except those corresponding to risk factors and assumptions about how inputs and risks relate to the final result. In other words, you're plugging ideal execution into the real world, with its real risks and real strategic relationships.

Once you've made the substitutions, you can estimate what you and your team should have accomplished by adjusting the actual final result so it bears the same relation to your input assumptions as the actual final result bears to actual input levels. Your execution gap is the difference between this estimate and the final result.

To estimate your uncontrollable gap, you need to determine what you and your team should have accomplished if you were right about the risk factors you've identified in your key unsettled assumptions. Substitute your projections or estimates for those risk factors into the relationship you've just used to estimate your execution gap. The implied final result shifts again, and the new shift reflects your uncontrollable gap.

The readjusted final result is also the goal you should have projected or set given your risk assumptions. The difference between it and the final goal you initially set is your strategy gap. (You get three gaps from two sets of substitutions for the same reason you get three pieces by slicing what's left of last night's pie twice.[9]) You may want to check whether the outcomes of the remaining indicators—the ones reflecting any assumptions you've made about how inputs and risks relate to your final result—explain your entire strategy gap. They should if you've found the correct overall relationship.

Here's a simple example that may be reminiscent of Cisco's inventory travails in 2000. Imagine you are the general manager of that division that makes airframes. The standard price is, say, $2 million. You hope to contribute $8 million to operating profits for the month by selling forty airframes that cost $1.8 million each. You ask procurement to do its best on unit costs. Let's assume that the complex resins needed for these bodies must be used immediately or written off.

At the end of the month, you find you've sold thirty-six airframes. Procurement reports a cost of just $1.7 million per frame—but you earned only $4 million. It turns out that procurement locked itself into a contract for the material for forty airframes regardless of actual sales. Without orders for the leftover material, you cannot make use of it.

The pattern of gaps depends on what exactly you asked procurement to do. Suppose you asked procurement to minimize cost per frame without regard to the number of frames sold. Then you would calculate the execution gap by substituting your cost assumption of $1.8 million per frame into what actually happened. You would have earned revenue from thirty-six frames for $2 million each less the cost of material for forty frames at the assumed level of $1.8 each rather than the actual level of $1.7 million each—for an adjusted break-even result. Since you actually earned $4 million, procurement did better than you assumed—albeit through contract terms that increased risk. But given what you asked procurement to do, the execution gap—$4 million of overperformance—shouldn't reflect any losses from the unused material. This case illustrates that there can be advantageous gaps when results are better than you expected.

Now substitute your risk factor assumption into the scenario. Substituting the sales assumption of forty airframes, here treated as a risk factor, for the actual sales of thirty-six airframes, you would have earned revenue from forty airframes for $2 million each less the cost of forty airframes for $1.8 million each—for a readjusted result of $8 million. This differs by $8 million from what procurement would have achieved if it had negotiated only the expected unit cost in its unfortunate fixed-volume contract. The uncontrollable gap is $8 million to your disadvantage.

It's true that procurement overperformed on its narrow goal of cost per frame by $4 million, but the effect was to increase your exposure greatly to the risk of poor sales, which in this case opened an $8 million uncontrollable gap. These two gaps fully account for your $4 million shortfall since there's no strategy gap in this example.

Now let's say you'd given procurement the broader goal of minimizing actual unit costs. In other words, procurement is responsible for the purchase of unusable material. You will still substitute your $1.8 million unit cost assumption into what actually happened, but you will also substitute the assumption that procurement pays for no more material than you use. You would have earned revenue from thirty-six frames for $2 million each at a cost of $1.8 million each, or $7.2 million. Since you actually earned $4 million, the execution gap is $3.2 million. The uncontrollable gap is $0.8 million, reflecting the fact that you earned your expected margin on just thirty-six rather than forty airframes.

Unlike the first case, the second case's execution margin accounts for most of the $4 million performance shortfall compared to your planning assumptions. This makes sense, since here you asked procurement to take into account the total effect of its contract regardless of how sales turned out. That wasn't so in the first case.

Although there's no strategy gap in this example, you could easily think of the oversight about fixed-amount contracts as a strategic error. The last step focuses on what to do about all three kinds of gaps, especially uncontrollable ones.

Step 3: Evolve Your Assumptions

At one level, this final step is easy. It's time to revise your plans in the light of your most recent performance experience, and you'll need to make up a new list of key assumptions that reflect your thinking. But we've already covered how to select and formulate assumptions, so this step is really just a reminder to go back to Chapters One and Two and start the process again. That wouldn't do justice to what you've learned by splitting performance surprises into strategy, uncontrollable, and execution gaps, however. This is no idle exercise. It gives concrete direction to problem solving about performance.

Strategy gaps, for example, measure the impact of flaws in your plans. They focus your attention on finding better ways to hit your goals. They can equally well reflect flaws in goals imposed on you. Organizations that pursue stretch goals for performance will routinely generate strategy gaps. Since those gaps ascribe performance shortfalls to flaws in the assumptions behind the goals rather than execution, they appropriately focus attention on the goal-setting process.

The next section goes into a little more detail on ways to prompt creative thinking. For now, it's worth bearing in mind that strategy gaps are not a sign of failure. They are why we have our jobs. Only new and creative assumptions, which may always be mistaken, can help us find ways to reduce strategy gaps. And creative assumptions are one thing that no automated planning program or business analytical engine can supply.

Execution gaps reflect flaws in assumptions we've made about the resources and inputs that will be at our disposal to reach a goal. Much of the time, we've agreed on these assumptions with colleagues or teammates as their final goals. So execution gaps can indicate problems others must solve to close their own strategy gaps.

It goes without saying, of course, that execution gaps won't absolve you of responsibility for a performance surprise. But they provide a fair standard of accountability for your team because they exclude the effect of planning errors and risk factors outside your team's control.

Moreover, the balance of strategy and execution gaps tells you where the problems are that need the most attention. If you have persistently high strategy and low execution gaps, you may want to promote a staff member to help you manage the sources of strategic uncertainty. If you have persistently low strategy and high execution gaps, you may want to take a close look at the upstream operations generating unstable results.

Uncontrollable gaps reflect flaws in your assumptions about risk factors you've already identified. These are the known unknowns. Sizable uncontrollable gaps may indicate a need for better forecasting or the impossibility of predicting the risk factor in question. What's important about an uncontrollable gap is its pattern or distribution.

In effect, your organization should be able to set a limit on the probability of missing a goal. For example, it may ask all executives to manage to a standard of hitting their goals 99 percent of the time. That standard will determine the organization's credit rating. You must manage your operations so that you can hit your goal with that probability regardless of the outcome of any risk factor. That may force you to aim for an average result substantially higher than the goal. Your pattern of uncontrollable gaps tells you how much higher. When risk factors become so unstable that we must raise our targets to inefficient levels, we have to find ways to mitigate or avoid those risk factors.

What about all the unidentified risk factors that beset our jobs? They register in our strategy and execution gaps. You can think of a search for ways to close a mysteriously variable strategy gap as the search for an unidentified risk factor. This is one of the most valuable disciplines imposed by a strategy review. It lets you transform strategy gaps into uncontrollable gaps—but only after you identify and find a way to measure the risk factor. The same is true of unstable execution gaps. Once you and your staff identify a source of instability in execution, you can isolate your execution gaps from its effect—but only after finding a way to measure it.

Whether you identify risk factors underlying your strategy gaps or your execution gaps, the effect of defining uncontrollable gaps for them is the same. You will have to hit your goals some percentage of the time regardless of the outcome of those risk factors. Whether you do so by aiming high or avoiding the risks becomes the next issue.

How to Close a Strategy Gap

So far my advice for closing a strategy gap—like the advice for whichever colleague is responsible for some part of an execution gap—is to be creative. Being creative may be a requirement for closing a strategy gap, but it hardly tells you how to close it. I'm at risk of substituting a requirement for a prescription, an ingredient for a recipe. No wonder it's so hard to define testable strategies using balanced scorecards!

The bad news is that there is no guaranteed cure for a strategy gap. There are lots of things we don't know about the universe, and one of them is what's missing from our mental model of how our business, agency, or nonprofit mission works. The good news is that there is endless scope in any field of activity to try new things and learn.

If that sounds too optimistic, consider exactly how often you would have used a flush toilet or suffered dysentery if you were born a hundred years ago. Or imagine how you would have collaborated with remote colleagues on a report fifteen years ago. The effect of cumulative learning is overwhelming. That's probably the central message of this book. Setting up your planning and performance system to learn from mistaken assumptions may look like a losing proposition over the next performance period, but it is the only proven way to make progress over many iterations and longer periods of time.

The implication for closing strategy gaps is to try new stuff. One of the most effective devices I've seen for generating new strategic ideas is profit redenomination. Jim Collins describes it in his deservedly popular book *From Good to Great*. He writes (his italics), *"If you could pick one and only one ratio—profit per x (or, in the social sector, cash flow per x)—to systematically increase over time, what x would have the greatest and most sustainable impact on your economic engine?"*[10] His best examples include Abbott Lab's shift from profit per product line to profit per employee, which motivated a move into simpler products. Gillette moved from profit per division to profit per customer, focusing the firm on the value of repeat purchases. Kimberly-Clark made a transition from return on assets to profit per brand, driving its transition from forest products to consumer products. Walgreens moved from profit per store to profit per customer, highlighting the premium its customers placed on convenient location. And Wells Fargo shifted from profit per loan to profit per employee, anticipating the rise of fee-based services in banking.[11]

While Collins goes into little detail about profit redenomination, I believe it identifies a fundamental step in creatively rethinking strategic assumptions. I think he's stumbled on a way of eliminating conflicts between strategy and execution.

The denominators of striking profit ratios tend to be key targets of management attention. That's true of Abbott's and Wells Fargo's employees, Gillette's and Walgreens' repeat customers, and Kimberly-Clark's brands. Think of them in general terms as critical aspects of execution. The ratios themselves reflect key strategic assumptions about the economics of the business. So in a very basic sense, the denominators reflect critical elements of execution, while the ratios reflect critical strategic assumptions.

The striking thing about the profit ratios Collins identifies is that they didn't necessarily fall—in fact, some rose—as his case companies increased their denominators. In the classic example of scale economies, the key profit ratio might be profit per unit sold. But that ratio rises with an increase in units sold under true economies of scale. Since the product of units and profit per unit is total profit, that's good news.

It would have been hard to increase Abbott's product lines indefinitely, for example, without suffering deteriorating profit per line. No such conflict arises with the firm's new focus of attention on profit per employee. This is even clearer for the former profit per division target at Gillette, where each division needs to incur new acquisition costs for the same customer that do not arise for a single division's replacement parts.

Similarly, the growth of old paper mill assets at Kimberly-Clark could only erode its prior target of returns on assets. The conflict does not arise with profit per brand, where brand proliferation in the company's consumer sector increases customer awareness and eases procurement by customers like hospitals.

Perhaps the best example of conflict between strategy and execution arose from Walgreens' prior focus on profit per store since it implied evenly spaced locations, as Collins points out. With even spacing, however, there's a limit on how many new stores you can add in general and not sacrifice per-store profits. The firm's new profit-per-customer target quickly reveals that no such conflict arises for clusters of urban stores. Urban customers will pay a premium to be able to dash into a familiar retailer on any street corner and find just what they expect.

In other words, profit redenomination is a powerful discipline. It gets you to compare the profitability of different elements of what you manage. And it pushes you toward the profitability targets that you can raise even as you increase or intensify the base on which they're measured. That's rare. More of an input usually reduces its profitability, and that means conflict with any strategy targeting its profitability. In the terms of this chapter, strategy and execution gaps tend to narrow only at one another's expense. I might make the execution of a quality program more predictable by simplifying and standardizing the products I manufacture, for example, but only at the price of making the response of diverse customers—a strategic assumption—less predictable. Profit redenomination, on the other hand, searches for goals that don't set execution and strategy in conflict.

So think of the various factors that contribute or add up to success at your organization: divisions, regions, customers, segments, assets, sales, employees, transactions, branches or stores, product lines, goods delivered, projects completed, time, and so on. And ask whether the profitability of any of these factors—Collins' profitability per x—might keep rising as you increase or intensify the factor. If so, you may find yourself on the road to a productive strategic shift.

The same reasoning applies to an execution gap. The difference is that you will often have delegated at least partial responsibility for closing the execution gaps you measure. Regardless of who leads the problem solving, however, the idea behind profit redenomination may apply, even if it's no longer profit that you need to redenominate.

Say that you rely on a quality department to minimize defects in workshop drills that you make and sell. And suppose the performance of the drill business you run is suffering from a rise in defects, which shows up as an execution gap when you conduct a strategy review of results for the past month. Your quality officer sees your execution gap, denominated in dollars, as a strategy gap for which he is responsible, denominated in some measure of defects. It may make sense for your quality officer to start thinking about various factors affecting defects: employees, hours, production lines, and so forth. The question is whether he can continuously reduce—not increase!—any of those measures of defects even while raising or intensifying the corresponding factor.

One big clue to the cause of a strategy or execution gap, naturally, will be the outcomes you compare with your projections or expectations for the indicators testing each of your key assumptions. If there is a glaring difference between your expectation and the actual outcome for an indicator, at least one of your assumptions is in trouble.

Strangely enough, you won't always be sure which one. Despite all of the care you may take to find indicators relevant to each of your assumptions, you can never be absolutely sure which of your assumptions is responsible for a performance shortfall. You may always be missing an assumption, for example, that would strengthen one that appears weak and cast doubt on another that looks stronger in the light of actual results.

Assumptions operate together as a network to yield expectations much as the parts of a scientific theory or the definitions of foreign words work together to help us interpret lab results or sentences of unfamiliar languages. Here are a language example and a business example to illustrate the problem. The examples also suggest a solution.

Suppose you're learning German in Munich, and you assume the German word for traffic light is the same as the German word for fire. When someone behind you shoves you at a street corner, you try to say that the light is red: "*Der Feuer ist rot.*"

Unbeknown to you, the person who pushed you has just seen a small yellow (not red) blaze spring from a nearby trash can and wants to get away from the corner. She remarks in German, "I wouldn't say that," and moves quickly on. You scratch your head and cross the street without ever noticing the fire.[12]

Although you chose a fairly good test for your assumption that *Feuer* means traffic light, you mistakenly conclude from the miscommunication that you're wrong. This is just like a situation where you've missed a performance goal, and a surprising outcome for the indicator you're using to test a new business assumption convinces you wrongly that the assumption is responsible.

Several years ago, for example, I thought treasurers of leveraged companies could make especially good use of research into widely shared challenges in managing bank lenders. The Corporate Executive Board program I ran for treasurers wrote a study on the subject and tracked new subscribers by amount of leverage. Surprisingly, the study proved just as popular among cash-rich treasurers as among heavy borrowers. It wasn't until years later, when researchers in the program designed a great online tool to help treasurers juggle bank relationships, that the original assumption proved true. What I was missing was an assumption about the kind of issues treasurers can more readily approach through tools than studies.

As a practical matter, you'll know whether you've thrown out a good assumption because you missed a hidden one. Future results will betray the error. The German speaker, for example, will eventually learn that he was right about the word for traffic lights and wonder what was going on at that street corner.

The advantage of strategy reviews is that they contain the problem. The relevance screen in Chapter Four gives a good reason to toss out an assumption when its indicator surprises you. By definition, you've chosen the indicator because a surprising result would be even more shocking if the underlying assumption were true. So you toss out the assumption and devise a new one. But you can never be sure you're right—even about tossing an assumption. That's okay; future strategy reviews will revisit the issue if your strategy gaps don't stabilize. The advantage of this approach to planning lies not in some elusive promise of infallibility but rather in helping you learn about strategy over time and avoiding threats to organizational morale and solidarity as you do so.

Trust and Risk

The biggest benefit of strategy reviews is motivational. Organizations that don't look for strategy errors in their performance results force their operating managers to protect themselves from being blamed for missing unrealistic goals, and that usually means sandbagging performance projections.

Think of the last time a boss, CEO, or board of directors handed you a goal you didn't think was reasonable. Where did that target come from? Why should you respect it? Whoever handed you the goal probably arrived at it by working backward from an investor, donor, or political requirement. Isn't that simply arbitrary?

The sense of being a victim of arbitrary targets becomes even sharper if you're working alongside colleagues whose goals seem much easier to achieve. In that case, promotion to a limited pool of more senior positions may be at stake. And yet you're stuck at the low end of an uneven playing field.

Of course, there is no such thing as a purely rational goal. You might think you could set a rational goal for a business process that you and your team understood completely. But no matter how well you understand a process, there's always room to improve on it. Stretch goals are probably the best way to force you and your team to find those improvements, and stretch goals are not purely rational.

There is a way to make goals objective, however: you can exploit the fact that it's often easy to tell when a goal is mistaken even if you can rarely be sure that a goal is exactly right. That's why confidence grows over time in any series of goals subject to routine criticism. Substituting theories for goals, Stephen Jay Gould wrote, "Objectivity cannot be equated with mental blankness; rather, objectivity resides in recognizing your preferences and then subjecting them to especially harsh scrutiny—and also in a willingness to revise or abandon your theories when the tests fail (as they usually do)."[13]

In other words, all you need to do is make sure the goals in question are subject to critical review. By separating strategy gaps from execution gaps, of course, that's what strategy reviews try to accomplish. And they're not hard to implement. Yet strategy reviews like the ones described in this chapter are still quite rare.

The reason may be that organizations get stuck in a vicious cycle. It starts with an erosion of confidence in goals when reviews of performance results neglect the possibility of strategic goal-setting errors. Morale declines, and operating managers naturally try to protect themselves from unrealistic targets. It's no secret how to do that. If your performance results are consistent, it will be hard for your CEO or board of directors to set standards that diverge from them. And if you aim for a target that's safely inside your operation's capabilities, you can expect to hit it consistently. As a result, the organization starts performing predictably—by stalling.

Ironically, operating inside your capabilities can raise risk. Experience becomes useless if it just keeps confirming that you can hit a safe goal. You won't have to stay on top of how the challenges to your business, mandate, or mission are changing. And you'll be more likely to miss early warnings of big changes.

Chrysler, McDonnell Douglas, and Sears each lost their independence three to five years after they stopped contending the leadership of their sectors.[14] Dogmatic, top-down goal-setting characterizes each of the cases.

Boeing acquired McDonnell Douglas three years after CEO John McDonnell turned the controls to Harry Stonecipher in 1994. When Stonecipher said, "We're going to merge our way out or sell our way out," almost from the start, he seemed to signal that the venerable company was in a holding pattern until something happened, and it did.[15]

Chrysler collapsed into Daimler's arms under CEO Robert Eaton five years after Lee Iacocca got bored with it in 1993. Breezily assuming 15 percent growth overseas "for the foreseeable future," the five-year plan Eaton drew up in 1992 looked more like a sales brochure for the business than a keen-eyed appraisal of challenges and capabilities.[16]

And K-Mart acquired Sears five years after CEO Arthur Martinez passed the baton to forty-six-year-old credit executive Alan Lacy in 2000, essentially declaring the old retail empire a credit company. Companies seem to shrivel when like Sears they stop exploring the limits of their operating capabilities. Incidentally, the merger came two years after the board cut Lacy's bonus in half for failing to meet a preestablished earnings-per-share target.[17]

If operating inside your capabilities creates risk and if ignoring goal-setting errors leads managers to operate inside their capabilities, what's gained by ignoring goal-setting errors? Presumably you avoid the embarrassment of recognizing strategic missteps. But it's unclear that Wall Street punishes those missteps any differently from other kinds of problems. So organizations that don't recognize the role of strategic errors in performance shortfalls end up transforming the narrow risk of admitting planning errors into a wider risk of deteriorating performance and stalled growth.

As growth stalls, most organizations start performing more detailed requirements analyses to reignite it. That would be fine if requirements told you how to achieve a growth target, but they don't. Since there are endless different ways to specify possible requirements, however, such organizations develop an insatiable demand for more data.

The victimized operating manager isn't blameless in this vicious cycle either. Faced on the one hand with goals that seem arbitrary but no one confronts, and on the other hand with the availability of reams of data, what do you do? You ask for measures of risk factors that might at least explain a performance shortfall.

This is a big deal. As financial executives install enterprise-wide planning systems, operating managers are deluging them with requests for data on profitability and risk factors. The problem is that while CFOs and controllers complain about all the requests for new indicators that they receive, they rarely ask their business partners to forecast them. It seems like a little thing, but it clouds performance further.

Suppose you ask for data on the profitability of your brown-eyed and blue-eyed customers. At the end of the month, let's say April, your CFO tells you that brown-eyed customers are worth ten dollars each and blue-eyed ones are worth five dollars. She also tells you that you made only 85 percent of your operating profit goal for April. You claim that you would have done things differently had you known those profitability numbers.

At the end of May, the profitability report shows that brown-eyed customers are worth twelve dollars and blue-eyed ones just four dollars. Your CFO says, "Looks like the profitability report isn't doing much good."

"Are you kidding?" you reply. "We would have had a terrible month without that report."

"But you're still at 85 percent of goal," she points out flatly.

"Sure," you say, "but I didn't know brown eyes would be worth twelve dollars instead of ten dollars."

Your CFO's problem is that she doesn't have a clue whether you even assumed the May profitability figures would be the same as April's, and she won't know your assumptions about June either unless she asks. Without your forecast of critical data you use in running your operations, there's no way to tell whether future problems stem from wrong assumptions about how the data have changed or from how you reacted.

The broader lesson is that data cannot fully support operating decisions unless we make some record of how we expect the numbers to change. Data without forecasts hang out there as possible excuses for performance shortfalls—call them exculpatory metrics. By themselves, however, they cannot reveal whether we know how to use them.

Completing the vicious cycle, your CFO can no longer be sure whether your beliefs about key factors or your responses to changes in them account for your performance results. As your performance results become more opaque, your boss, CEO, or board of directors may try to prescribe operating requirements more precisely. The performance system tracks more operating indicators. You ask for more profitability and risk indicators. Trust erodes in both directions. And the organization compensates by seeking more data.

But if you had to limit your data requests to indicators you were willing to forecast, you would quickly focus on the most critical unsettled assumptions you have to make to run your operations. In other words, you would be using performance data to test your own strategic assumptions and would be implementing the guess-test performance system in this book. And you might even focus your boss, CEO, or board of directors on making goal-setting assumptions fairer by testing them explicitly.

6

PLANNING TO EVOLVE

We won't really be able to learn from experience, according to Chapter Five, unless we use operating results to test our key strategic assumptions. This chapter takes that idea one step further and projects it into the future. It argues that our organizations won't sustain growth unless we use the pattern of gaps in our performance results to review strategy and revise tactics continuously. It's the strongest claim in the book.

The first section of this chapter illustrates why the pattern—and especially the variability—of gaps in performance results is so important for managing growth and risk. That pattern compresses your organization's performance experience into three numbers. The variability in your execution gaps reveals volatility in your operations that you and your colleagues should be able to control. The variability in your uncontrollable gaps shows how risky your current strategy is. And your strategy gap variability shows whether you understand your operations well enough to set fair goals and sustain growth. Together these numbers tell you where to focus your attention as a manager.

If sustained growth really requires the continuous revision of tactics in the light of performance experience, argues the second section, Nestlé must be doing it. The Swiss company manages to sustain above-average growth in food even though it's the largest player in a notoriously sluggish business. As it turns out, gaps in performance results lie at the heart of Nestlé's performance system. The system balances the stretch in the goals of short-term regional strategies and longer-term product strategies that those gaps reflect so their variability across products and regions becomes informative even within a single performance period.

Nestlé's regional and brand strategies thus evolve in response to the full variety of its experience in emerging and developed markets throughout the world.

The pattern of gaps in performance results provides an answer in the third section to questions about the optimal frequency of performance data updates and reviews. That pattern tells you whether you need to focus on solving execution or strategy problems. While your organization's response time determines the optimal frequency of execution-driven reviews, the relevance of available performance results drives the optimal frequency of strategy-driven reviews. The section introduces metrics matrix time tracks to help you determine the relevance of hourly, daily, weekly, monthly, and quarterly results from a performance indicator to any strategic assumption you need to check.

The final section makes the case that sustainable growth ultimately requires even variability in your execution, uncontrollable, and strategy gaps. Even variability means that you and your colleagues are solving execution, risk, and strategy problems at the same rate. In other words, you've managed to coordinate problem solving.

The idea of even gap variability has three important implications. First, it provides a rule of thumb for allocating your time and that of your colleagues to performance problems that should coordinate problem-solving efforts across your organization without a formal project management structure. Second, it reveals which units in your organization could operate independently—that is, which units' performance results are mostly irrelevant to one another's strategic assumptions. This delivers on the promise made earlier to show how relevance affects the optimal scope of a firm. Finally, it provides a baseline allocation of management responsibilities that distributes performance challenges evenly. Such a baseline lets you check the fairness of your organization's incentive compensation by comparing the skew in top management compensation with the skew—compared to the baseline—in its responsibilities.

In sum, the chapter outlines a relevance revolution in how to use information to manage and organize. The variability of execution, uncontrollable, and strategy gaps in the performance results most relevant to our key strategic assumptions can shake up ineffective approaches to planning and organizational learning. By telling us which of our assumptions are most in need of repair—execution, risk, or strategy—the pattern of those gaps lets us allocate scarce talent to our most persistent problems. The result is a fully engaged management team that evolves strategy continuously by testing its strategic assumptions in parallel and revising the weakest ones. Those assumptions—the guesses of the guess-test system—largely replace formal planning. We will still plan, but only to evolve.

The Pattern of Gaps in Performance Results as Keys to Managing Growth and Risk

The pattern of gaps yielded by strategy reviews over time compresses your organization's most valuable asset—its performance experience—into three numbers. The variability in your execution gaps reveals volatility in your operations that you and your colleagues should be able to control. The variability in your uncontrollable gaps shows how risky your current strategy is. And your strategy gap variability shows whether you understand your operations well enough to set fair goals and sustain growth. Together these numbers tell you where to focus your attention as a manager.

Variability of Execution Gaps

Execution gap variability is the most familiar of the three. By *variability*, I mean the typical deviation of your execution gaps from their trend.[1] It's familiar because most businesses that track the accuracy of their performance forecasts assume variances are simply execution gaps. They trace performance surprises to execution as if risk factors and goal-setting assumptions played no part. While they often ignore uncontrollable gaps and almost always ignore strategy gaps, in other words, they never ignore execution gaps.

In a performance system that pulls apart these three sources of surprises, however, execution gaps are especially powerful. First, they avoid giving your team the impression of arbitrariness since they try to separate goal-setting mistakes from pure execution problems. By tracking their variability, moreover, you can start to tell whether execution problems stem from consistent overoptimism or a deeper misunderstanding.

As the head of national sales for a farm equipment manufacturer, for example, imagine you consistently miss your top monthly sales goal by $5 million. And say $4 million of the shortfall arises because your team consistently misses its conversion rate goal—its goal for converting prospects into customers—by 2 percent.

In one respect, this isn't such bad news, and the low variability of the $4 million execution gap—the gap due to missing your conversion rate assumption—reflects it. Plenty of managers intentionally run consistent execution gaps by setting stretch goals for things their staff control. Where members of the team set their own consistently overoptimistic goals, it may be enough to ask them to improve their forecasts.

But if your execution gaps jump all over the place from month to month, there's a problem with some aspect of the resources or operations on which you rely. The assumptions underlying the gaps should point out the source of instability and even the team members or colleagues who need help. And your team's or colleagues' assumptions may pinpoint the problem. In particular, they should be able to tell whether the problem lies with their own strategic assumptions, the execution factors they control, or the risk factors they don't control.

For example, you may find that sales reps have trouble predicting how many customers will cancel their orders because the reps can't guarantee delivery when a customer wants it. In this case, the variability of your execution gaps probably reflects a combination of strategy (overpromising), uncontrollable (demand volatility), and execution (inventory reporting) problems from the sales reps' point of view. An answer may be to make sure the sales team works more closely with inventory control.

In other cases, the answer may be to identify new risk factors and try to forecast and measure them. If a new risk factor helps explain performance surprises, it will increase the variability of your uncontrollable gaps. And your execution gap variability will decline by a similar amount, reflecting a better understanding of what your team controls and what's uncontrollable. So let's turn to instability in uncontrollable gaps.

Variability of Uncontrollable Gaps

Uncontrollable gap variability focuses you on a different kind of problem: whether it's worth offsetting a risk. In the case of farm equipment sales, for example, commodity prices can be a huge risk factor. When those prices rise, farmers are flush, your sales team closes a lot of business, and you risk running out of inventory. When those prices fall, business is scarce, and you risk an expensive inventory overhang. You can estimate your worst-case losses due to commodity price volatility from its effect on your uncontrollable gaps. And that tells you the value of offsetting it.

The first step here is projecting commodity prices. The forecasts can be as simple as taking the previous month's closing price. For instance, you might assume that corn prices will continue at $4.25 per bushel and your sales will reach $100 million for the month—only to see prices fall to $4.00 per bushel and sales fall to $80 million. The point is that your baseline assumption for the effect of commodity prices on results lets you relate surprises in results to surprises in commodity prices. This is another example of the rule of thumb that you should measure only what you're willing to forecast.

Tracking the impact of commodity prices on your uncontrollable gaps over time tells you what their unpredictability costs.

Here's how you can estimate it. Set a confidence standard such as 99 percent. List your monthly uncontrollable gaps (or the part of them due to commodity prices) from lowest to highest, and then read off the gap that's worse than 99 percent of the list but less than the other 1 percent. The answer is the cost to you of commodity price unpredictability at a 99 percent confidence level. It basically puts a cap on losses due to commodity price surprises that you can promise your CEO or board of directors you'll exceed no more than 1 percent of the time.

Once you have that cost, you can determine the best way to handle the risk it reflects. Suppose your CEO wants you to guarantee you'll hit your $100 million monthly sales goal 99 percent of the time regardless of commodity prices. And say your uncontrollable gaps due to commodity prices exceed $3 million just 1 percent of the time. First, estimate the cost of building up the sales team to hit a goal of $103 million—so you have confidence that commodity price surprises will push you below $100 million only 1 percent of the time. Next, estimate the cost and practicality of hedging commodity prices. Then compare them.

This is a classic trade-off that operating managers face every day. To be confident of meeting a goal, is it better to aim a lot higher than the goal or reduce the variability of your results? Uncontrollable gap variability tells you how much higher you must aim so you can compare the cost of raising your goal with the cost of hedging.

In this example, the pattern of gaps would also help you determine whether it's worth changing your business mix or redesigning your sales model. You might, for instance, change the mix of equipment you sell. Suppose you estimated you could sell $105 million per month of a different mix of tractors. But you also thought your worst-case uncontrollable gaps would rise to, say, $10 million. The new mix would not let you hit your $100 million goal within your CEO's or board's appetite for risk.

More important than what the pattern of your uncontrollable gaps lets you do, ironically, may be what it protects you from doing.

Uncontrollable gaps require risk factor forecasts or at least explicit assumptions about key risk factors. And those explicit assumptions or forecasts keep you from falling into the predictive metrics trap.

The predictive metrics trap is a natural one. We all have a rough mental model of how our jobs and organizations work. That is, we have a sense of what kind of results we're after and what factors can affect them. We control some of those factors; some are uncontrollable. So it's natural, when work surprises us, to look for factors that can explain the surprises. After collecting a lot of demographic data on your customers, for example, you may find you can explain 75 percent of the differences in their profitability. What about the remaining 25 percent? Since income data might explain it, you want a new indicator for customer income. It's natural to think of such an indicator as a predictor. In fact, operating managers nearly always seem to be looking for predictive metrics.

The trouble is that they usually don't predict anything in the sense of foretelling it. Simply put, if you have data for all the important factors affecting your results for the month of July, you should have a good sense of your July results. What those data do not give you is a good sense of your August results.

This is a puzzle if you've just missed your July numbers. You know predictive metrics help you understand your business. After all, they can often explain why you've missed a target. How can they do that without providing a little foresight? Aren't predictive metrics the same as leading indicators?

Truly predictive metrics are indeed leading indicators but they are rarely interesting. Most of the so-called predictive metrics we track, analyze, and dispute are really explanatory metrics. They help predict results in the sense of explaining them, but they do so only for the period in which you measure them. They're absolutely central in knowing what matters—but not by telling the future.

Explanatory metrics test your key assumptions. They improve your future decisions only indirectly by helping you understand your past ones—by learning from experience or, if you prefer, driving through the rearview mirror. Looking for

metrics that are predictive in this sense of the term is natural—
it's part of the process of sharpening your assumptions.

Leading indicators, however, do say something about the
future. But they're rarely all that interesting. The reason is that
at any point in time, we've long ago factored them into our current plans. Like demographics, they long ago defined our baseline
expectations. The latest figures for a leading indicator may help us
plan for next year but by definition won't change our minds about
running things better right now.

More interesting are the new factors that change the effect of
leading indicators in the moment. For example, housing starts may
be a good leading indicator of house sales, but real estate agents
rarely find themselves poring over last quarter's housing starts.
What they want to know is how the economy might affect current
sales. What they want, in other words, is to refine their understanding of how housing starts drive sales. But that's a role for an
explanatory metric, not a predictive one.

The predictive metrics trap is another search for magical
data—this time, for data to foretell the future. Every now and
then, we discover a new leading indicator, keeping alive our hopes
for better foresight. But even when we find one, we quickly factor
it into our baseline expectations and forget about it—it becomes
a settled assumption. The danger here is that we'll forget what
makes our best metrics, and especially our risk factor metrics,
valuable. Their real value is their power to improve gradually our
understanding of our jobs and organizations by explaining what
just happened.

Variability of Strategy Gaps

Consistent strategy gaps, like consistent execution gaps, aren't
necessarily bad news. As we saw in Chapter Three, they're probably an unavoidable part of learning for any organization trying
to grow since it's hard to grow if you don't set stretch goals. But
having no strategy gap may be a sign that your organization or

institution is not trying to grow at all. After all, you can always eliminate strategy gaps by negotiating goals you're sure of meeting. Consistent strategy gaps may be better than none.

It's inconsistency in your strategy gaps that signals a problem—and specifically a flaw in your strategic assumptions. There could be an important unidentified risk factor. Or there could be an input or controllable factor creating more instability in results than the ones you've identified. Either way, you must make an assumption about the new factor and test it by looking for a relevant metric that you can forecast and measure.

If the new factor really matters, it will transfer some of the variability of your strategy gaps to your execution or uncontrollable gaps. This is progress: you've identified a risk or an operational issue that someone needs to manage. Bearing the new factor in mind, you will be in a position to set goals more fairly. You've gained insight into your operations, which is just what greater strategy gap stability indicates.

As head of national sales for the farm equipment manufacturer, for example, say your monthly strategy gap is quite low on average—maybe $1 million—but highly variable—typically deviating perhaps $4 million from that average. This means your list of critical unsettled assumptions is missing an important source of variability. After reviewing your operations, you might identify a new risk factor—the price of corn—and a new execution or controllable factor—sales force discipline in keeping inventory control informed about the order book. You formulate assumptions about the impact of these factors, you start to forecast and track corn prices, and you define a metric for communicating orders to inventory control that you can forecast and measure.

Suppose, as a result, you find your execution gap variability rising by $2 million, your uncontrollable gap variability rising by $2 million, and your strategy gap variability falling by $3 million.[2] You're now in a position to focus on what to do about corn price exposure and cooperation between sales and inventory control. And you can have greater confidence in the sales goals you negotiate with your CEO.

Much of the time, however, there is no single risk or execution factor to be discovered that will tame a series of highly variable strategy gaps. Strategy gap variability often means you just need a better way of thinking about how to achieve your goals. In fact, that's the reason for both the brevity and flexibility of the eight-line strategies described in Chapter Two. In principle, you should be willing to rethink your assumptions every time results surprise you—or at least whenever your strategy gap variability shows that even the surprises are surprising. If rethinking your assumptions means reprogramming a fourteen-page planning model, you won't do it very often. But if it means reviewing an eight-line strategy, you're more likely to rebuild your top-line model of the business whenever it breaks down.

The section in Chapter Five on closing strategy gaps applies equally to the challenge of reducing their variability. The method of profit redenomination it proposes is a simple way to force yourself to rethink how your part of your organization achieves its goals. Its advantage is that it will get you to reconsider all of your key working assumptions as a group rather than one by one. That's especially important when there's no obvious weak link in an eight-line strategy.

Variability of Peer Organizations' and Competitors' Strategy Gaps

What happens when an organization does not react to variability in its strategy gaps? After all, few organizations think of performance surprises systematically in terms of execution, uncontrollable, and strategy gaps.[3] Fewer still estimate how much of their performance unpredictability comes from their strategy and goal-setting errors. All most organizations know is that their goals are hard to hit.

Persistent strategy gap variability stalls growth. This is because it reveals a failure to find assumptions that reflect reality more closely. You might think strategy gap variability could simply reflect business risks. But as long as you can identify the sources of those risks, your uncontrollable gaps—and not your strategy gaps—will pick up their impact on the unpredictability of your results. So volatile strategy gaps mean you're not revising flawed assumptions or, for some reason, rarely finding better ones.

But why must a series of bad assumptions hurt growth? If an organization faces a growth stall, for example, it must have had decent growth in the past. Is there any reason to think it operated with better strategic assumptions while it was growing? If not, might great assumptions be helpful but not absolutely necessary for growth?

It's true that a management team can sustain growth despite unrealistic assumptions about its business if it faces little competition. As falling communication costs make global competition possible, however, few uncompetitive industries and nonprofit sectors remain. Competitors matter. They'll exploit any bad assumptions you're making if they can. And even if they can't, they'll make some of your assumptions obsolete just by changing the environment in which you operate.

This, presumably, is why business success reflects how much faster you update your business model than your competitors do. It's as if an accelerating arms race in organizational learning were forcing us to shift our attention from comprehensive but irrelevant management reports to the efficient testing of creative, changing, and ever more incisive assumptions about what drives our businesses. Strategy gap variability is a direct measure of how well we do that.

It's possible to get a rough sense of the size of the strategy gaps of many publicly traded firms from public data. You can estimate the variability of their strategy gaps by calculating the standard deviation of the difference between their earnings per share projections and whatever consensus analyst earnings estimates you can find for recent quarters from providers like Thomson Financial. I recommend looking for management and analyst projections about six months before the quarter in question and examining at least five years of quarters if possible.

This method is fairly easy, but it makes a heroic assumption: that analysts have correct business models for the firms they cover, better even than the business models of those firms' executives. This is rarely true. Often, however, analysts have fewer reasons to be biased in their earnings projections, and when that's the case, the difference between analyst and management estimates of a firm's results will yield something that resembles a strategy gap.

In practice, I've found that the availability of public earnings guidance announcements from management teams constrains this kind of analysis. Larger firms tend to have more consistent records of announcements, so the greater numbers of quarters for which you can estimate their strategy gaps make those gaps appear less volatile than those of smaller firms.[4] Nevertheless, it's a start at understanding how quickly firms within a sector are learning about changing business conditions.

Learning Continuously to Sell Chocolate Everywhere

Patterns of execution gaps, uncontrollable gaps, and strategy gaps show you how to allocate scarce talent evenly across the challenges your division or organization faces. Without any formal project structure, the gaps basically let your management team engage in parallel efforts to solve the most serious problems underlying your current strategy. They let your organization revise tactics continuously for growth.

Nestlé sustains above-average growth in food even though it's the largest player in a notoriously sluggish business. If sustained growth really requires the continuous revision of tactics in the light of performance experience, Nestlé must be doing it. As it turns out, gaps in performance results lie at the heart of Nestlé's performance system. The system balances the stretch in the goals of short-term regional strategies and longer-term product strategies that those gaps reflect, so their variability across products and regions becomes informative even within a single performance period. Most firms can compare gaps meaningfully only in individual businesses' performance over time.

Packaged foods tend to grow about as fast as global population does. And sector leaders tend to grow more slowly than smaller upstarts because it is so hard to accelerate large corporate ships. Nevertheless, Nestlé's ten-year growth, excluding acquisitions and divestitures, has been 5.4 percent per year. That compares favorably with Unilever's 2.9 percent and Cadbury Schweppes' 3.4 percent, and not badly with smaller rival Groupe Danone's 5.5 percent.[5] How has Nestlé kept growing?

Of the firm's threefold growth in market value from 1997 to 2000, retiring CEO Peter Brabeck said, "We see adapting, improving, and restructuring as a continuous process. . . . Evolution can happen if you believe in it. . . . It happened without frenzy, without bloodshed. Just constantly challenging people to be better, day by day, bit by bit."[6] The keys to this quote are Brabeck's references to growth as an evolutionary process and to the idea of continuous challenge.

Nestlé's group controller, Jean-Daniel Luthi, explains that the company's focus is on the gaps between forecast strategic goals and actual performance rather than traditional long-term planning. Normally the thousands of combinations of brands and markets in which Nestlé operates would draw specific product market forecasts and goals of widely varying feasibility, or what I'll call stretch. So it would normally be necessary to track gaps in those local product markets over a period of time to generate the kind of insights that the previous section extracts from measures of gap variability. Luthi and his colleagues have found a way, however, to make sure that the feasibility or stretch in local market goals is roughly comparable across products. That makes the pattern of hits and misses across those markets meaningful even within a single performance period.

Luthi has a keen sense of just how hard that challenge has been given the enormous differences across Nestle's markets around the world. He recalls rebuilding Nestlé's Indonesian operations in 1971 at a factory for condensed milk in the port city of Surabaya in eastern Java.[7] There was no telephone, so communication with the outside world was possible only by coded telex to Jakarta, and then only when an executive secretary stationed in Jakarta could get through to Switzerland. He spent an entire day buying forty liters of milk in local markets—only to find it had spoiled. Developing comparably realistic expectations for Nestlé's hundreds of products in markets sometimes as different as Surabaya and Switzerland is no trivial task.

Nestlé assigns responsibility for long-term product development goals to strategic business units housing its major brands. And it assigns responsibility for shorter-term sales and margin growth to geographical units called zones. This in itself is an interesting practice, though hardly unique to Nestlé. It achieves the balanced scorecard's aim of reminding us to look after things that take time, like talent development.

It also achieves the strategy review's aim of separating execution errors from errors in strategic assumptions and goals. To the extent the zones' short-term sales goals function as operating assumptions in the brand managers' longer-term strategies, surprises in regional results resemble execution gaps, and those in brand results resemble strategy gaps. Nestlé can thus test the validity of its longer-term strategies and its short-term success in carrying them out at the same time.

The zones prepare market development programs based on all of the strategic business units' global brand strategies. The programs typically involve market prices, volume targets, and levels of various categories of expenditures. The zones and strategic business units then negotiate unified, end-to-end projections incorporating agreed goals across products and markets.[8] It's these negotiations that are distinctive at Nestlé.

The effect of the negotiations is to distribute the stretch in the firm's overall goals for sales, profits, and spending evenly across local product markets. Suppose, for example, that Zone Asia thinks it can do better with Nescafé in Vietnam than Nescafé's strategic business unit expects but not as well as expected with Nescafé in Indonesia. Just shifting Nescafé resources (like advertising) from Indonesia to Vietnam may not make sense given the total sales goals for those countries across all Nestlé products, however. Regional managers could look for a different product—say, the KitKats that Nestlé makes and distributes outside the United States—that had more potential to beat expectations in Indonesia than in Vietnam. KitKat and Nescafé adjustments might offset one another.

As strategic business units negotiate to protect their long-term brand plans and zones negotiate to protect their shorter-term country plans, consensus targets for local product markets emerge. Those targets still add up to totals that are consistent with the firm's brand and regional plans, but now they should reflect comparable ambition.[9]

Whenever a zone misses a goal or a strategic business unit undergoes a change in competitive position, Nestlé reviews its strategy and updates its tactics. In particular, it compares the gaps in regional market results and the gaps in global product results. To the extent the negotiations across products and regions transmit the stretch in Nestlé's goals evenly across those product markets, the gaps tell a lot about the accuracy of the brand and regional managers' assumptions. For example, they might show that growth assumptions for Nescafé and KitKat should be further apart for Indonesia and that those for Vietnam should be closer together.

In sum, equal stretch in Nestlé's regional and product goals lets Nestlé compare performance gaps for different products and markets the way most firms can compare only the gaps for individual product markets over time. Wide variations across gaps within a single period reveal more at Nestlé because the firm's extensive negotiations between product and regional market managers make them more surprising.

It's no coincidence that the focus on missed goals resembles Toyota's fallibilism. As Peter Brabeck says, "The biggest problem with a successful company is that you don't learn from success."[10] Nestlé's global brands and regional strategies evolve continuously in response to the full variety—and especially to what's surprising about the variety—of its experience in emerging and developed markets around the world every day.

Metrics Matrix Time Tracks and the Frequency of Performance Updates

What's the optimal frequency of performance data updates and strategy reviews? The pattern of gaps in your performance results tells you whether you need to focus more on solving execution or strategy problems. While your organization's response time determines the optimal frequency of execution-driven reviews, it's the relevance of available performance results that drives the optimal frequency of strategy-driven reviews. This section introduces metrics matrix time tracks to help you determine the relevance of hourly, daily, weekly, monthly, and quarterly results from a performance indicator to any strategic assumption you need to check.

Execution-Driven Reviews

The response time of your division or organization places a limit on how frequently you can usefully update performance indicators and review strategy. In fact, a lot of variability in execution gaps may suggest you aren't giving your teams enough time to try out alternative ways to deliver on their operating promises.

Suppose you run a custom package delivery service for valuable shipments. You know what kind of on-time delivery rates you need to maintain to compete in a tough market. And yet your delivery teams keep delivering too many packages a little late. So you embark on a series of one-month experiments that vary delivery truck scheduling, package registration procedures, service levels, and so on. Yet after six months, your on-time delivery execution gaps remain stubbornly variable. No matter what you do, on-time rates vary chaotically.

The problem may be that your one-month experiments are too short. If you run two-month experiments instead, you might find that one of the experiments produces better and more stable on-time delivery rates. And the only way to find out may be to try experiments of different duration. In this example, you might mix up one-month and two-month experiments to see whether the longer experiments result in less variable execution gaps. If so, your operation's response time is longer than a single month.

You face a choice whenever you determine that response time constraints are contributing to volatile execution gaps. One option, taken in the package delivery manager example, is to change tactics less often. The other is to try to speed up response times. That's beyond the scope of this book. Nevertheless, operations analysts often say that recognizing a response-time constraint is half the battle.

Strategy-Driven Reviews

Just as response-time constraints can make execution gaps more volatile, poor data can make strategy gaps more volatile. After all, variable strategy gaps indicate stubborn problems with your strategic and goal-setting assumptions. That's not always for lack of creativity in devising new ones. Sometimes it reflects statistical volatility in the metrics you use to test those assumptions.

To continue with the previous example, say you decide to track the daily number of late deliveries, defined as those made four hours past their promised arrival time. Suppose deliveries that late don't happen every day, so if you looked at a week of daily late delivery tallies, it wouldn't be surprising if they bounced around a lot—perhaps five in one day and none in another. They might bounce around enough to convince you of the instability of a process affecting on-time delivery that's actually stable.

Conversely, you might have a lot of days without late deliveries despite an on-time delivery problem. In this case, your teams might have streaks of late delivery days. But since you're tracking late deliveries every day, things might appear to be under control most of the time. Either way, your daily late delivery metric is misleading.

A solution is to track on-time deliveries by tallying weekly or even monthly late deliveries. The counts will be higher. So the law of large numbers should reduce the noise in your results to the variability of the underlying process. In other words, variability in an indicator tracking large numbers of events suggests that an unstable factor—and not just a statistical fluke—is at work.

You can use the metrics matrix from Chapter Four to compare these update frequencies. For example, Figure 6.1 compares daily, weekly, and monthly late delivery indicators. In this example, the daily tally lacks not only specificity but also relevance. That's because the indicator's relatively low counts make an occasional outlying result unsurprising even if the on-time delivery process really is under control.

Here, weekly and monthly counts are high enough to be relevant, but monthly counts offer more detail. Their greater specificity reflects the higher counts of late deliveries typical of whole months. If your weekly count varied between fifteen and twenty, for instance, you might expect a monthly count to vary over a wider range, like fifty to one hundred. The monthly indicator has higher specificity since it has more possible outcomes.

Figure 6.1 Metric Matrix Time Tracks: On-Time Delivery

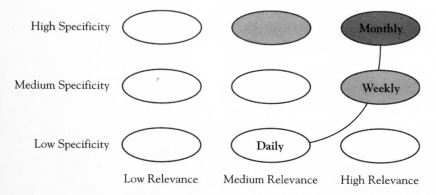

You can determine how frequently to update an indicator by looking to see what frequencies land it in the upper-right part of a metrics matrix. You may want to link the positions occupied by the same indicator over different periods of time with an arc to make them easier to read and interpret. In fact, you could compare several competing quality indicators with different periods or update frequencies on the same matrix. You could compare late delivery counts with tallies of customer complaints, for example, to see how frequently you would need to update each one to produce a decent service quality metric.

What should you do if some of your indicators require more frequent updating than others? Many executives consider it a best practice to update each key performance indicator only as often as necessary. While that seems like a good way to reduce performance management costs, though, I think it can lead to trouble. To see why, imagine you're an operations manager at an airline, and you track seven or eight key service quality and customer satisfaction indicators every week. One of your indicators, however, is costly to collect that often—say, the number of times customers switch flights at the airport. So you compile that indicator monthly.

Suppose a key performance indicator like percentage of occupied seats starts to slip the week after you update your customer switch metric. One problem is that you won't know for another three weeks whether customer switches are moving in the same direction as occupied seats. But the worse problem is that you're limited in the kind of fast experiments you can run to find out what's happening.

You might want to offer more discounts for people who keep their original reservations or raise penalties for those who switch at the last minute. But you'll need to compare the benefits of the discounts or penalties in terms of reduced customer switching with the cost in terms of more customers who fly with a competitor. The problem is that you can't measure those benefits until the end of the month at the earliest even though you might track the costs right away. You'll lose time while results deteriorate.

More broadly, you can never be sure which of your key assumptions may be responsible for a performance surprise. Sometimes it's obvious, but not always. And the whole point of tracking performance results is to take nothing for granted. Where possible, therefore, it makes sense to update all of your key metrics at once. In particular, it may be worth spending a little extra to update an indicator that's hard to refresh as frequently as the others you track.

Self-Organized Coordination, the Optimal Scope of the Firm, and the Fairness of Compensation

This section makes the case that sustainable growth ultimately requires even variability in your execution, uncontrollable, and strategy gaps. *Even variability* means that you and your colleagues are solving execution, risk, and strategy problems at the same rate. In other words, you've managed to coordinate your problem solving.

The idea of even gap variability has three important implications. First, it provides a rule of thumb for allocating you and your colleagues' time to performance problems that should coordinate problem-solving efforts across your organization without a formal project management structure. Second, it reveals which units in your organization could operate independently—that is, which units' performance results are mostly irrelevant to one another's strategic assumptions. This delivers on the promise made earlier to show how relevance affects the optimal scope of a firm. Finally, it provides a baseline allocation of management responsibilities that distributes performance challenges evenly. Such a baseline lets you check the fairness of your organization's incentive compensation by comparing the skew in top management compensation with the skew—compared to the baseline—in its responsibilities.

Self-Organized Coordination

What can the pattern of gaps in your performance results tell you about your organization's structure? Balance in your execution, uncontrollable, and strategy gap variability basically reflects a healthy division of labor in your organization. To see why, look at each of the cases where one kind of gap variability dominates the others.

If your execution gaps are more variable than your uncontrollable and strategy gaps, you need to stabilize some aspect of execution on which you've been relying for results. The simplest case is where the job of someone reporting to you has grown more complex than your own. If your job is to coordinate sales and inventory control, for example, and inventory control generates most of your problems, maybe you should focus on inventory control and not worry about the sales side of coordination.

If your uncontrollable gaps are more variable than the others, you are responsible for results driven mostly by a risk factor. Since the risk factor is uncontrollable by definition, all you can do is mitigate it, work around it, or set a level of expectations high enough to clear your goal most of the time in spite of it. But all too often we convince ourselves we can somehow manage stochastic processes. We let ourselves become spear-catchers instead of clearly communicating what we don't know to our colleagues.

If your strategy gaps are more variable than the others, you're having trouble explaining surprises that occur even when the controllable and uncontrollable factors you've identified are predictable. Your job is basically too complex, especially compared to colleagues reporting to you who are responsible for execution. It may make sense to break apart the strategic challenges you face and promote some of those colleagues to help manage them. Alternatively, you may have an underworked boss who can help.

Now imagine that all the managers in your organization calculate the variability of their execution, uncontrollable, and strategy gaps. Imagine that they shift responsibilities to staff where strategy gaps dominate, redefine positions that sit helplessly on top of uncontrollable risk factors, and pick up staff responsibilities where execution gaps dominate. A more even allocation of business problems across the management team will necessarily emerge, and you'll be solving them in tandem.

What you and your colleagues will have coordinated isn't so much a novel business process as attention to the biggest challenges your organization faces. And you'll have done it without any meetings or disruptive special projects.

One way to get there from wherever you're starting is simply to start tracking gap variability in your own performance results. It doesn't matter whether anyone else in your organization does so. The simplicity of the methods in this book—eight-line strategies, the metrics matrix, and strategy reviews—guarantees that if they help you, your colleagues will be interested. And as the Nestlé example shows, payoffs grow as more people in your organization put them to work. Problems will naturally distribute themselves across your management network.

The Impact of Relevance on the Optimal Scope of the Firm

What should you conclude if there's no significant strategy gap at the top of your organization? Perhaps your firm misses its numbers from time to time, but only because of well-defined risks and controllable factors, not because of strategy errors. There are two possibilities. One is that the head of the organization is clairvoyant and never makes a mistake. The other is that the units reporting to the head of the organization run independently in the sense that their experiences are not relevant to one another.

Either way, the head of your organization has a good job—perhaps too good a job. If there really are no errors in strategic assumptions, the CEO's lieutenants are doing all of the ongoing work. And if the units run independently, the CEO is redundant. Look for a private equity firm to buy her out of the picture and save costs.

The key, as I've argued throughout this book, is relevance. If two divisions report to you and each one benefits from lessons learned by the other, you have a real job—and it's the job of a teacher. It isn't so much a matter of making sure managers reporting to you share best practices as making sure they share worst ones.

They'll benefit because the results of each division are relevant to the key unsettled assumptions of the other.

You can tell right away that they'll benefit from one another's experience if their eight-line strategies or key performance indicators are similar. But they may benefit even when they share no assumptions or metrics. In general, two divisions will benefit from one another's experience—and from common management—when at least one of their key indicators scores well on a metrics matrix for the assumptions of the other. But if none of their indicators tests any of the other's assumptions, the combination is sterile. A breakup may be in order (so long as they can do business efficiently at arm's length) because there's no reason to pool their experience.

The Fairness of Compensation

Most of the complexities of compensation go beyond the scope of this book. But there's one contribution that the pattern of gaps in an organization's performance results can make to questions about pay. Human resources and finance executives occasionally need to check whether their executive compensation levels make sense. The variability of executives' strategy and execution gaps sheds light on the question.

You may ask why the question even arises. After all, markets set compensation levels. But those are markets for the skills of individuals. No job persistently puts all of our skills to work, so there's a real issue whether the problems that a given position calls on an executive to solve are worth the market rate for that executive's skills. And there can be a question whether differences in the problems executives are solving justify differences in their pay.

To get a handle on the latter question, you can compare the variability of a given executive's strategy and execution gaps. If his strategy gap variability is negligible, his job may no longer be generating sufficiently complex problems to justify his compensation; worse, he may be bored. It's a sign that the job should be redefined. Conversely, if his strategy gap is much more variable than his execution gap, he may be undercompensated compared to the managers working for him. The reason is that his managers are, by definition, overseeing processes that are fairly predictable.

But how can you tell whether the variability in his strategy gap reflects job complexity or simply a failure to find effective solutions? At the end of the day, it's profitability that justifies persistent volatility in performance results and hence in strategy gap variability. Financial theory suggests that the market should set a clear rate between the rate of return on investment in an operation and its market risk.[11] You don't need to know what that rate is to compare the strategy gap variability of different executives with the profit contribution of the divisions they run. You would expect the highest-paid executives to preside over units contributing the most profit with correspondingly high strategy gap variability. Anomalies—highly paid executives with low strategy gap variability and the reverse—may be worth a look.

The larger lesson here is that the variability of strategy and execution gaps measures something like the intensity of outstanding management challenges. It doesn't reflect current work effort so much as work effort needed. As a prospective measure of future problems to be solved, however, it may help define the value of a job.

Here, in sum, is the outline of a relevance revolution in how we use information to manage and organize. The variability of execution, uncontrollable, and strategy gaps in the performance results most relevant to our key strategic assumptions are tremors that can shake up ineffective approaches to planning and organizational learning. By telling us whether our assumptions about execution, risk, or strategy are most in need of repair, this pattern of gaps lets us allocate scarce talent to our most persistent problems. The result is a fully engaged management team that evolves strategy continuously by testing its strategic assumptions in parallel and revising the weakest ones. Those assumptions—the guesses of the guess-test system—largely replace formal planning. We will still plan, but only to evolve.

Conclusion

THE BEGINNING OF THE RELEVANCE REVOLUTION

If it's true that the information revolution has generated piles of data so complex we can hardly tell what matters, how are we to learn from experience going forward? This book argues we must use performance results to sharpen strategy instead of pursuing them—under the banner of great execution—solely as ends in themselves. Sharpening strategy through performance results basically requires three things: the development of performance strategies explicit enough to be testable, the derivation of performance metrics from the assumptions behind those strategies, and the use of performance gaps to reveal errors in goals and assumptions as well as execution.

Learning from experience starts with performance strategies explicit enough to be testable. A strategy is testable if it spells out goals and assumptions about how to achieve them that could conceivably prove wrong. Chapter Two proposes eight-line strategies for distilling the strategy relevant to a manager at any level of an organization to a short list of testable assumptions. Laying the foundation for vastly simplified management reporting and performance reviews, these assumptions let you pick out the facts most relevant to your strategy from large amounts of conflicting performance data.

To learn from experience despite the noise of that conflicting data, you should derive your performance indicators from those strategic assumptions—and not from balanced lists of output targets and input requirements. Chapter Four defines the relevance of a performance indicator with respect to assumptions about what will achieve a strategy's goals. A performance indicator is relevant to a strategic assumption, according to the definition, if the assumption's truth or falsity greatly affects the results you expect.

Requiring only a pen and piece of paper, the metrics matrix proposed in Chapter Four uses this definition to determine what indicator best tests each of your key assumptions from an eight-line strategy. The indicators on the resulting list are the only ones you need to track until your strategy changes. Balanced scorecards, in contrast, rarely test strategies. They have a natural tendency to test something quite different: requirements for success. The problem is that you can meet a list of requirements and still miss the goal. Since there is no end to the requirements you can identify, balanced scorecards tend to accumulate more and more metrics without ever defining a testable strategy.

To learn from increasingly complex experience, finally, we must use performance gaps to reveal errors in our goals and assumptions as well as in execution. Splitting the difference between actual and expected performance results into execution, uncontrollable, and strategy gaps, Chapter Five proposes a model strategy review that explicitly challenges strategic plans and assumptions in place of traditional reviews of performance results that focus only on execution. Strategy reviews look at every performance period as a controlled experiment. These experiments naturally test work effort and risk forecasts, but they also test the quality of the assumptions relating that effort and those forecasts to results. The biggest benefit of strategy reviews is motivational because organizations that don't look systematically for strategy errors in their performance results force their operating managers to protect themselves from being blamed for missing unrealistic goals.

Our organizations won't sustain growth, furthermore, unless we use the pattern of gaps in our performance results to review strategy and revise tactics continuously. That pattern compresses your organization's performance experience into three numbers. By telling you which assumptions—about execution, risk, or strategy—are most in need of repair, the pattern of gaps lets you allocate scarce talent to your most persistent problems.

The result is a fully engaged management team that evolves strategy continuously by testing and revising assumptions at every level of the organization.

This book aims at the broad problem of knowing what matters in the face of overwhelming amounts of conflicting data. It's a problem that we face in our households, neighborhoods, schools, charities, and circles of friends as well as in our workplaces. I've addressed it by working out a solution in the specific context of improving organizational performance. One reason is that today's organizations are some of the worst culprits in generating reams of data. The other is that challenges in improving organizational performance force you to explore nearly every corner of the broader problem of learning from collective experience.

I hope nonbusiness readers benefit from this approach. Even if you're trying to get better results from your church's next fund drive or make a positive change in your dating life, the book's fundamental approach should be relevant. Make plans that are testable in the sense of being explicit enough to be mistaken. Focus on the most likely signs of error. And pursue results for the sake of learning rather than just vacuous success. If the fallibilism that these principles embody is a touchstone for business progress, it must be just as important to our private lives.

However applicable this approach may be to the general problem of learning from complex experience, some of its implications for organizational performance are especially striking. Here, in closing, are the ones that have most surprised me in developing it.

1. How Is Organizational Learning Related to Growth?

Now that consultants are making money from business analytics software, there's no shortage of arguments that learning promotes growth. After all, information advantages and disadvantages have come to define the front lines of business competition. If you can learn about a customer need, emerging vendor, or new technology faster than your competitors can, you may capture an insurmountable share of the market.

More interesting is the idea that growth promotes learning—and that learning may be a reason for pursuing growth. The idea, adapted from virology, is that the quick strategy iterations required for growth make you learn more about which variations work, and the stress that growth puts on a strategy reveals hidden flaws faster. Your strategy, as a result, becomes more resilient: it won't crumble the moment competition heats up. So growth, which usually comes at the price of risk, can actually reduce it when we open our strategies to continuous critical review.

2. What's Wrong with Balanced Scorecards, and What's the Alternative?

It's too easy for organizations to fill out balanced scorecards with lists of obvious requirements for success that resemble ingredients in a cookbook. The trouble isn't that the ingredients may be wrong; it's that they run so little risk of being wrong. As a result, they end up saying very little.

This isn't what Kaplan and Norton, the designers of the balanced scorecard, intended. They meant to coax users into balancing the shorter-term financial and customer satisfaction goals with the longer-term process and capability requirements of their framework. Since nothing in the framework forces users to specify a strategy for achieving their goals that's specific enough to be wrong, however, most users stick to requirements that tell you little about how to achieve them.

The alternative would be a planning and performance system based on your biggest bets about how to achieve a financial or market objective. These assumptions are more like recipes than lists of ingredients. They specify how to achieve an objective, may be wrong, and require testing and revision. But they focus you on the performance results from which you can learn the most—about your current strategy.

Call the alternative the *guess-test* performance system—in contrast to *analyze-execute* processes that try to derive strategy from the raw data of a comprehensive scorecard and test only whether execution is faithful to it. While guesses in the form of assumptions may seem like a strange place to start learning from experience, the emphasis on testing strategy rapidly homes them in on the realities of your business. And all that testing reminds you every business plan is fallible.

3. How Should We Set Performance Goals?

We should separate performance goals that test strategy from incentive goals that determine compensation. Unless we're really paycheck-driven machines uninterested in whether our strategies are right, these two kinds of goals serve different purposes.

To test strategy, performance goals need to express the most precise possible expectations. This means performance goals should be short-term indicators of long-term progress, and you should have a 50 percent chance of hitting them. If you set only long-term goals, you'll learn nothing from your results until too much time has passed to change course. And if you set goals at levels other than what you expect—the 50 percent mark—you won't really test the expectation. So what I'm calling performance goals will usually be considerably harder to hit than incentive goals.

It also means you probably shouldn't set operating goals by reasoning backward from investor expectations about returns or earnings per share. If you do, you're probably calculating operating requirements—necessary conditions—for hitting your financial target. But requirements don't tell you how to hit a financial target, and meeting them won't guarantee that you'll hit it. In the end, requirements are no substitute for a strategy that can ensure you'll achieve a financial target and operating goals that embody that strategy.

4. How Do Testable Strategies Help Us Learn from Experience?

Testable strategies are the key to experimental management, and experimental management is the key to adapting to changing business or security environments. Experimental management uses performance results to test strategy the way lab results test scientific theories. The point is to find the best current theory of your business.

To find the best current theory, focus on where your current strategy might most go wrong. That would be in one or more of your biggest bets or high-surprise assumptions—the ones that are highly uncertain and have a big impact on expected results. A list of those assumptions is a good summary of what's worth testing in your current strategy. In fact, a testable strategy is nothing more than such a list.

If you're focusing on high-surprise assumptions, you can keep the list short. You'll want to include an assumption for your final results—that's almost always uncertain—as well as assumptions for the most volatile factors you control, the biggest risks you've identified, and the spillover effects you most want to avoid.

Since each of the assumptions on the resulting list is uncertain and each one has a practical impact on expected results, each one should be testable and you should be able to find an indicator that could reveal its flaws. Of course, you won't be able to test your strategy if it changes too frequently—that is, if it's chaotic. And you won't be able to test it if its expectations lie too far in the future—in cases where it's free to stagnate. But if you can effect changes in your strategic assumptions as frequently as you can test them, your performance results should quickly guide you to a fit strategy.

This may sound so reasonable it hardly seems worth the argument. And yet few countries in the world pursue testable diplomatic strategies regarding something as vital as security. Although U.S. and European strategies toward the Middle East keep failing, for example, they never seem to change. The reason may well be that we base diplomacy in the area on assumptions about intentions so broad that no finding or news item could ever disprove them. Such strategies fail to evolve precisely because they are untestable.

5. Which Metrics Matter?

The metrics that matter are the ones that are relevant to assumptions that matter. And the assumptions that matter, as I have argued, are the ones that are uncertain and have the biggest impact on expected final results.

Many managers seem to be either overly optimistic or overly pessimistic about finding metrics relevant to their strategy. Overly optimistic managers find evidence that confirms their beliefs wherever they look—even where the evidence would be no more surprising if their assumptions were wrong. A good definition of relevance needs to guard against false positives.

Overly pessimistic managers despair of finding relevant metrics, so they try to find metrics for every aspect of their operations they can define. They inadvertently favor detail over relevance in the sense of the power to overturn strategic assumptions. The result is voluminous performance reports filled with conflicting answers to any question. Such reports generate more false negatives than truly relevant benchmarks do.

The best metric for testing a strategic assumption is both relevant—in the sense of avoiding false positives and negatives—and specific. Relevance makes sure your expectations are sensitive to the truth or falsity of the assumption. Specificity makes sure the metric really captures those expectations. Together, relevance and specificity reflect the real value of a metric for someone proceeding on the basis of the assumption.

The most important implication of this way of looking at metrics is that they should change. It's true that you should track consistent metrics for your final goals, such as profit, margin, economic profit, or return on assets, equity, or investment. But the metrics you use to test your assumptions about how to achieve those final goals need to change when the assumptions change. And if your metrics are doing any good at all, they occasionally overthrow an assumption and force you to make a change.

Risk managers may prefer long series of results from consistent metrics, but learning requires failed assumptions, and new assumptions require new metrics.

6. How Can We Measure Relevance?

It's possible to measure the relevance of a performance indicator, experience, or piece of news if you define it with respect to an assumption or a prediction. That may be controversial: we usually think of relevance as pertaining to problems or situations, not to our guesses about how to solve them. But it starts to make sense if you think of learning as a process of trial and error and indicators as ways of conducting trials.

The idea that you need to define relevance with respect to assumptions about how to solve a problem sheds light on search engines like Google. It shows that the relevance of search results for a user is no simple matter of understanding what problem the user is trying to solve. To assess relevance, you need to understand how the user is trying to solve the problem, and that requires live interaction.

It also sheds light on the editorial question about what stories will be most relevant to newspaper and Internet readers. Since relevance emphasizes the power of new evidence to overturn your assumptions, editors should run the stories likely to challenge most readers' preconceptions. That may seem to bias reporting toward bad news. But in fact it aims to maximize the usefulness of the news within the framework of expectations of most readers.

Here's a definition of *relevance:*

A performance indicator is relevant to a strategic assumption if the assumption's truth or falsity greatly affects the results you expect.

The results from an irrelevant indicator are equally likely whether your assumptions are true or false.

CONCLUSION: THE BEGINNING OF THE RELEVANCE REVOLUTION **183**

This definition is a marriage of several aspects of Bayesian probability and information theory. In essence, it picks out indicators for which your expectations are highly sensitive to the truth or falsity of competing assumptions. You can even quantify it by assessing how much your expectation about each possible result changes if you assume different underlying assumptions are true.

7. What Kinds of Acquisitions Are Relevant to Our Business?

From a learning perspective, the acid test for the relevance of two businesses is whether the results of one are relevant to the strategy of the other. If they are relevant, access to the experience of the first business can help the second one learn more and refine strategy faster. If they aren't relevant, the only benefit of merging the two businesses will probably be cost cutting. But between outsourcing, procurement alliances, and informal networks, mergers are rarely the only way to cut costs.

More broadly, relevance may define the ideal scope of a firm. This is a role that the potential for cutting cost through internal coordination used to play. If the divisions of your firm can realize lower costs through internal mandates than they would realize in the open market, according to a celebrated theorem of the economist Ronald Coase, they're better off together.

Since third-party services are now cutting the transaction costs of even the smallest companies, however, those costs no longer explain which firms should grow and which ones should not. But the internal relevance of business lines' results to one another's strategies can explain it. If the lines of business of your firm are able to learn from one another, they may be better off under a single holding company.

The idea that relevance, not transaction costs, determines the ideal scope of a firm has a startling implication: that a firm's ideal scope may change when its strategies change. While this idea would hardly justify the level and pricing of merger activity in

2007, it suggests that some of it may be rational for the moment. But deals that make sense given a firm's current strategy may make none under a subsequent one.

8. Are Forecasts Necessary?

Surprisingly, this book's perspective is that forecasts really are necessary. I call it surprising because a strong consensus has started to form that organizations should get rid of their annual budget process if they can. And many firms are replacing calendar-based forecasts with rolling ones that reforecast on a monthly basis the next year or year and a half of results. Since rolling forecasts readily dispense with any particular forecast, they give the impression that forecasts are not so important.

It's true that you can dispense with any given forecast as soon as you learn something about its accuracy. But it's only by confronting what you expect—your forecast, if you will—with a result that you can refine the assumptions behind your expectation. The whole point of measuring performance, on this view, is to compare it to a prior expectation that tests some part of your strategy.

This raises the question whether it's ever worth tracking an indicator if you aren't going to forecast or project its results at least informally. On this view, it makes no sense. Performance measurement is for learning, and learning means testing expectations. Performance measurement without some kind of forecast is like pitching without a strike zone. As one CFO put it, "Performance metrics without forecasts are harassment."[1]

9. Why Do Traditional Performance Reviews Destroy Morale?

Bad reviews are always demoralizing, but the idea that traditional performance reviews—even positive ones—systematically destroy morale is a much more serious charge. If performance reviews hold you accountable for gaps between goals and results regardless of the reasonableness of the goals, however, it's fairly compelling.

Goals, after all, are guesses. Your final goal—what you're ultimately supposed to deliver—is a guess about what you can achieve. That guess may be wrong, and if it's someone else's guess and it's too high, penalizing you for missing it is unfair.

What's needed is some sense of a reasonable expectation for what you can achieve. Any deviation in your goal from that reasonable expectation reflects an error in strategy. Any deviation from that reasonable expectation in what you achieve reflects an error in execution (or risk forecasting).

It's possible to go one step further, in fact, and split any difference between a final goal and a result into three parts: an execution gap for failures to meet expectations about factors you or your team control, an uncontrollable gap for mistaken expectations about risks you've identified, and a strategy gap for mistaken expectations about what you could achieve if all the assumptions about controllable factors and identified risks were right. Here are some more careful definitions of the three kinds of performance gap:

- Strategy gaps reflect the difference between the goal you set and the goal you should have set.
- Uncontrollable gaps reflect the difference between the goal you should have set given your assumptions about the risk factors you've identified and the result you and your team should have achieved given the way those risks turned out.
- Execution gaps reflect the difference between what you and your team should have achieved given the way the risk factors you've identified turned out and your actual final result.

Ideally every performance review would split apart these three kinds of gaps. That would ensure that we never held someone responsible for missing a goal when it was possible to criticize the reasonableness of the goal. And we would never hold people responsible for factors outside their control. Instead we would hold them responsible for what was most reasonable given our other assumptions. Let's call such three-way performance discussions *strategy reviews* to distinguish them from traditional performance reviews.

The strategy review's emphasis on checking goal-setting assumptions as well as execution might seem to contradict the spirit of stretch goals, which try to accelerate learning by challenging teams to sharpen their assumptions. The difference is that stretch goals ask you to find better ways to achieve results—changing other assumptions along the way. They ask you to aim higher.

Goal-setting errors ask for a result that proves impossible given the assumptions about controllable factors and risks underlying them. They ask you to shoot further without letting you aim higher. Stretch goals encourage creativity. Goal-setting errors reflect an inconsistency between inputs and outputs.

Strategy reviews have two enormous benefits and are much easier than commonly assumed. In one sense, the point of this book is to show how easy they are. You need just two things: (1) a list of your most important assumptions about a final goal and how to achieve it, including the most volatile controllable factors and biggest risks, and (2) specific indicators that are relevant to, in the sense of testing, each assumption.

The eight-line strategies and metrics matrix described in this book are just tools to generate the right kinds of assumptions and indicators. Once you have them, strategy reviews amount to a simple assessment of your assumptions in the light of actual results and an estimate of the contribution of errors in the different kinds of assumptions to the gap between your final goal and what you accomplished.

One big benefit of a strategy review is clarity about what kinds of problems you have to solve. Execution gaps require problem solving at the level of factors your organization controls. Uncontrollable gaps reflect challenges in risk assessment and mitigation.

And strategy gaps require you to rethink how those factors and risks relate to final results.

The larger benefit is objectivity and fairness about performance. By separating the effects of goal-setting errors and risk factor surprises from what a colleague controls, strategy reviews aim at a reasonable evaluation of her effort. And that means she has no need to protect herself from unreasonable expectations by projecting anything other than what she thinks she can deliver. The strategy review encourages an open exploration of what's possible for our organizations by criticizing the goals we set as well as what we do about achieving them.

10. What's the Relation Between Performance Volatility and Compensation?

We usually take performance volatility—measured by changes in the difference between goals and actual results from one period to the next—as a sign that a process is out of control, and that may lead to the process owner's loss of incentive compensation. But that's not the only way pay and performance volatility relate. By resolving performance volatility into the variability of each of the three kinds of performance gaps defined above, strategy reviews shed new light on compensation.

Variability in strategy, uncontrollable, and execution gaps helps locate the misunderstandings responsible for performance problems. If execution gaps are contributing the largest share of performance volatility, for example, then the owners of the processes underlying them may need more resources or management support. If your own strategy gap contributes the largest share, you may need help from your colleagues, teams, or boss with your own planning.

If everyone up and down your organization makes these kinds of adjustments, the variability in their strategy and execution gaps should start to even out. Even gaps reflect an even distribution of problems to be solved. By aiming for even variability in these gaps, you can effectively coordinate problem solving in your organization without any formal or cumbersome structure of tasks and projects.

These gaps also provide a perspective on compensation. It's reasonable to expect the executives with the largest problems to solve—presumably reflected in the variability of their strategy gaps—to receive the most compensation. Rough and preliminary statistical work suggests this is not often the case in large companies. If it turns out we are not compensating our top executives for the size and persistence of the problems they have to solve, there's a longer-term question about why we are compensating them. Strategy reviews provide a framework for starting to address this question.

11. What Does Relevance Have to Do with Leadership?

The guess-test performance system puts a premium on two contrasting—but not conflicting—styles of leadership. Boldness and clarity are crucial for the phase of learning from experience that emphasizes the clear articulation of assumptions and steady pursuit of the strategy they reflect. Skepticism and flexibility are crucial for the phase emphasizing the critical review and refinement of those assumptions in the light of results.

The 2004 U.S. presidential election provided a textbook case of the drawbacks of these two styles in isolation from one another. Democrats accused incumbent Republican president George W. Bush of dogmatism and reluctance to confront his assumptions with such results as the violent course of the Iraq war. Republicans pilloried Senator John Kerry, the Democratic challenger, for his lack of clarity on issues as central as that war. Many of those criticisms assumed that candidates who hedge their positions show a lack of resolve. In the context of guess-test learning, however, there's a deeper problem: if a leader pursues poorly defined policies, results won't reveal what doesn't work.

Yet the criticism of both candidates was wide of the mark. To manage through something as changeable as terrorist threats or a competitive business environment, a leader must both promulgate policies clear enough to test *and* be ready to change them. Clarity and a critical attitude are great virtues when combined. Instead of avoiding leaders with simplistic or nuanced approaches to the world, organizations and countries alike need leaders who alternate between them.

12. What's a Relevance Revolution?

Most revolutions define themselves by what they aim to follow, and the same is true of the relevance revolution sketched in this book. It aims to succeed an explosion in information resources—the information revolution—that has generated unprecedented detail and precision in the description of our business, strategic, and political environment. But because new technologies have greatly expanded the content or raw amount of information at our disposal, we have not worried too much about its relevance.

Now we find ourselves buried in factoids and cannot discern which data matter. We therefore find it hard to learn from the experience that our information systems so richly document. It's clear that the information we generate, for all its detail and specificity, often lacks the crucial ingredient of relevance. But efforts to define the relevance of that information to problems, situations, or conditions—mostly through intricate taxonomies of topical areas—have failed.

This book argues we must make a compromise with some of our cruder intuitions about objectivity to define relevance. We need to define it with respect to our guesses or assumptions about how to solve the problems before us and how to achieve the goals we've set. In other words, we must use our information resources to test our best current strategies and rely on those strategies' successors to explore the possibilities our earlier guesses may have ignored. We search possibilities with guesswork; we test guesses with crucial facts.

Relevance will engender a revolution because it relates the actual value of information to highly personal conjectures. For example, the same piece of information may have entirely different relevance to two people trying to solve the same problem in different ways. The value of information depends irreducibly on the user's assumptions.

The relevance revolution thus points to a fragmentation of information markets that will defy predictions of an analytical utopia waiting for those with the biggest computing networks and data warehouses. Creativity in laying out strategic assumptions and a readiness to test them with relevant indicators will matter far more to an organization's success than the size of its database and power of its analytical software.

The larger impact of the relevance revolution will be personal, however. The idea that information is relevant to the assumptions we make and not to the circumstances imposed on us is liberating. It frees us from a slavish attachment to the data and metrics that existing scorecards and planning software happen to accommodate. It gives us courage to stop looking for answers in the data at hand, however voluminous they may be, and start looking for whatever can test our most creative ideas.

Notes

Introduction

1. Cockpit transcript from T. N. Dunn, "The Tape They Wanted to Hide," *The Sun*, Feb. 6, 2007, retrieved June 21, 2007, from http://www.thesun.co.uk/article/0,2-2007060131,00.html.
2. R. Kaplan and D. Norton, "The Balanced Scorecard: Measures That Drive Performance," *Harvard Business Review*, Jan.-Feb. 1992, pp. 71–80. Also see R. Kaplan and D. Norton, *The Balanced Scorecard: Translating Strategy into Action* (Boston: Harvard Business School Press, 1996).
3. R. Rorty, *Objectivity, Relativism, and Truth* (Cambridge: Cambridge University Press, 1991), p. 31.

Chapter One

1. C. Woodyard, "Criticism Flies over BP's Pipeline Maintenance," *USA Today*, Aug. 8, 2006, retrieved Oct. 24, 2007, from http://www.usatoday.com/money/industries/energy/2006-08-08-pipeline-usat_x.htm.
2. R. Aronen, "BP's Bad News," *Motley Fool*, Aug. 7, 2007, retrieved Oct. 24, 2007, from http://aol.fool.com/news/mft/2006/mft06080714.htm.
3. S. Simpson, "BP: Bad Propane," *Motley Fool*, June 30, 2006, retrieved Oct. 24, 2007, from http://aol.fool.com/news/mft/2006/mft06063030.htm.
4. N. Adams, "The Marketplace Report: BP Oil Fined for Lax Safety," September 23, 2005, retrieved Oct. 24,

2007, from http://www.npr.org/templates/story/story.php?storyId=4860782.

5. F. Langfitt, "BP Refinery Accident Pinned on Equipment, Staffing," NPR, Oct. 31, 2006, retrieved Oct. 24, 2007, from http://www.npr.org/templates/story/story.php?storyId=6410203.

6. Langfitt, "BP Refinery Accident."

7. J. Roberts, *The Modern Firm* (New York: Oxford University Press, 2004), p. 183.

8. Roberts, *The Modern Firm*, p. 184.

9. Roberts, *The Modern Firm*, p. 186.

10. Roberts, *The Modern Firm*, p. 186.

11. Roberts, *The Modern Firm*, p. 112.

12. Roberts, *The Modern Firm*, pp. 188–189.

13. Roberts, *The Modern Firm*, p. 188.

14. "BP Failed on Safety, Report Says," *Washington Post,* Jan. 17, 2007, p. D2.

15. Mercer Human Resource Consulting is one example of a firm that regularly publishes the results of CEO pay surveys. Past surveys are available for a fee at http://www.mercer.com under "Surveys" and "Compensation."

16. R. Coase, "The Problem of Social Cost," *Journal of Law and Economics*, 1960, 3(1), 1–44.

17. R. Nelson and S. Winter, *An Evolutionary Theory of Economic Change* (Boston: Harvard University Press, 1982).

18. R. McGrath and I. MacMillan, "Discovery Driven Planning," *Harvard Business Review*, 1995, 7, 44–54.

19. "Paul O'Neill," *Wikipedia,* retrieved Oct. 24, 2007, from http://en.wikipedia.org/wiki/Paul_O%27Neill_%28cabinet_member%29.

20. P. More, "Scotiabank Commodity Price Index," Scotiabank Group, Dec. 21, 2006, retrieved Feb. 14, 2007, from http://www.scotiacapital.com/English/bns_econ/bnscomod.pdf.

21. D. Drickhamer, "Lean Manufacturing: The Third Generation," *Industry Week,* Jan. 3, 2004, retrieved Oct. 24, 2007,

from http://www.industryweek.com/CurrentArticles/ASP/articles.asp?ArticleId=1574.

22. Drickhamer, "Lean Manufacturing."

23. M. Tushman and C. O'Reilly, *Winning Through Innovation* (Boston: Harvard Business School Press, 1997), p. 50.

24. Tushman and O'Reilly, *Winning Through Innovation*, pp. 50–51.

25. Drickhamer, "Lean Manufacturing."

26. J. Dewar, C. Builder, W. Hix, and M. Levin, *Assumption-Based Planning: A Planning Tool for Very Uncertain Times* (Santa Monica, Calif.: Rand, 1993).

27. Dewar, Builder, Hix, and Levin, *Assumption-Based Planning*, p. xi.

28. Dewar, Builder, Hix, and Levin, *Assumption-Based Planning*, p. 5.

29. Dewar, Builder, Hix, and Levin, *Assumption-Based Planning*, p. 9.

30. Dewar, Builder, Hix, and Levin, *Assumption-Based Planning*, p. 7.

31. Dewar, Builder, Hix, and Levin, *Assumption-Based Planning*, p. 7.

32. Dewar, Builder, Hix, and Levin, *Assumption-Based Planning*, p. 13.

33. R. McGrath and I. MacMillan, *The Entrepreneurial Mindset* (Boston: Harvard Business School Press, 2000).

34. McGrath and MacMillan, *The Entrepreneurial Mindset*, p. 232.

35. McGrath and MacMillan, *The Entrepreneurial Mindset*, p. 233.

36. McGrath and MacMillan, "Discovery Driven Planning," pp. 44–54.

37. McGrath and MacMillan, *The Entrepreneurial Mindset*, p. 242.

38. McGrath and MacMillan, *The Entrepreneurial Mindset*, p. 243.

39. McGrath and MacMillan, *The Entrepreneurial Mindset*, p. 243.
40. P. Pande, R. Neuman, and R. Cavanagh, *The Six Sigma Way: How GE, Motorola, and Other Top Companies Are Honing Their Performance* (New York: McGraw-Hill, 2000).
41. It's on the order of one defect per 1 million.
42. C. Christensen, *The Innovator's Dilemma* (Boston: Harvard Business School Press, 1997).

Chapter Two

1. For the purposes of this book, *economic value added* means profit less a fair market estimate of the cost of required capital.
2. R. Kaplan and D. Norton, *Strategy Maps* (Boston: Harvard Business School Press, 2004).
3. Chris Morris, "The Case for XP," cLabs Papers, 2001, retrieved Oct. 24, 2007, from http://clabs.org/xpprac.htm.
4. See T. Cover and J. Thomas, *Elements of Information Theory* (Hoboken, N.J.: Wiley, 1991), p. 14. Example 2.1.1 shows the information content or entropy of a pass/fail variable is highest when the probability of passing or failing is one half.
5. This is really what risk managers mean by *value at risk*.
6. R. McGrath and I. MacMillan, *The Entrepreneurial Mindset* (Boston: Harvard Business School Press, 2000).
7. Kaplan and Norton, *Strategy Maps*, p. 228.
8. V. Pareto, *Cours d'économie politique professé à l'université de Lausanne* (Lausanne, 1896–1897).
9. Thanks to Joe Firestone of the Knowledge Management Consortium International for his focus on assumptions about side effects.
10. D. Apgar, *Risk Intelligence: Learning to Manage What We Don't Know* (Boston: Harvard Business School Press, 2006), p. 12.
11. See L. Bossidy, R. Charan, and C. Burck, *Execution: The Discipline of Getting Things Done* (New York: Crown Business, 2002).

12. This is called *supervenience*. Strategy is said to supervene on execution if any difference in strategy mirrors some difference in execution. It's like saying that strategy emerges from execution but without making any commitment about what causes what. The term arises from the mind/body debate and the argument that thoughts might supervene on physical states without reducing to them.

13. D. Davidson, *Truth, Language, and History* (Oxford: Clarendon Press, 2005), p. 200.

14. Sees K. Popper, *Conjectures and Refutations: The Growth of Scientific Knowledge* (New York: Basic Books, 1962).

15. K. Popper, *The Open Universe* (London: Routledge, 1988), pp. 41–42.

16. R. Dawkins, *Climbing Mount Improbable* (New York: Viking Press, 1996), pp. 70–71.

17. See, for example, E. Beinhocker, *The Origin of Wealth: Evolution, Complexity, and the Radical Remaking of Economics* (Boston: Harvard Business School Press, 2006).

Chapter Three

1. R. Kaplan and D. Norton, "The Balanced Scorecard: Measures That Drive Performance," *Harvard Business Review*, Jan.-Feb. 1992, pp. 71–80. Also see their *The Balanced Scorecard: Translating Strategy into Action* (Boston: Harvard Business School Press, 1996).

2. L. Serven, "Solutions for Better Planning: What a National Survey Reveals," Financial Executives Research Foundation, Jan. 2002.

3. C. Lewy and L. du Mee, "The Ten Commandments of Balanced Scorecard Implementation," *Management Control and Accounting*, Apr. 1998, cited in J. Firestone, "The Balanced Scorecard: Developments and Challenges," Adaptive Metrics Center, Oct. 9, 2006, retrieved Oct. 24, 2007, from

http://www.adaptivemetricscenter.com/media/BSCdevelop
mentsandchallenges.pdf.

4. K. Hendricks, L. Menor, and C. Wiedman, "The Balanced Scorecard: To Adopt or Not to Adopt?" *Ivey Business Journal*, http://www.iveybusinessjournal.com/view_article. asp?intArticle_ID=527, cited in Firestone, "The Balanced Scorecard."

5. D. Apgar, "Risk Intelligence and the Iraq War," *Globalist*, Sept. 14, 2006, http://www.theglobalist.com/StoryId. aspx?StoryId=5627 for Part 1 and http://www.theglobalist. com/DBWeb/printStoryId.aspx?StoryId=5628 for Part 2.

6. Apgar, "Risk Intelligence and the Iraq War."

7. R. Kaplan and D. Norton, *Strategy Maps* (Boston: Harvard Business School Press, 2004), p. 407.

8. Kaplan and Norton, *Strategy Maps*.

9. Kaplan and Norton, *Strategy Maps*.

10. R. McChesney, "FCC Scandal Explodes with Second Revelation of Suppressed Media Ownership. Research," CommonDreams.org, Sept. 19, 2006, retrieved Oct. 24, 2007, from http://www.commondreams.org/views06/0919–27.htm.

11. Kaplan and Norton, *Strategy Maps*, p. 406.

12. McChesney, "FCC Scandal Explodes."

13. Kaplan and Norton, *Strategy Maps*, pp. 157–160.

14. Kaplan and Norton, *Strategy Maps*, p. 159.

15. Kaplan and Norton, *Strategy Maps*, p. 160.

16. Kaplan and Norton, *Strategy Maps*, p. 161.

17. K. Goldman, *Conflicting Accounts* (New York: Simon & Schuster, 1996).

18. J. Jones, "Look What We Did," *Guardian*, Mar. 31, 2003, p. 2.

19. K. Roberts, *Lovemarks: The Future Beyond Brands* (New York: powerHouse Books, 2004). Kevin Roberts, *The Lovemark Effect: Winning the Consumer Revolution* (New York: powerHouse Books, 2006).

20. Kaplan and Norton, *Strategy Maps*, p. 314.

21. Kaplan and Norton, *Strategy Maps*, p. 314.

22. Kaplan and Norton, *Strategy Maps*, p. 314.
23. D. Qingfen, "Continental Shift," *China Daily*, Mar. 13, 2006, retrieved Oct. 24, 2007, from http://www.chinadaily.com.cn/english/doc/2006–03/13/content_533447.htm.
24. D. Qingfen, "Continental Shift."
25. D. Qingfen, "Continental Shift."

Chapter Four

1. Author interviews on Mar. 1, 2007, with former Capital One business analyst Darrin Howell and on Jan. 26, 2007, with former Capital One treasurer Susanna Tisa.
2. J. Hammond, R. Keeney, and H. Raiffa, "The Hidden Traps in Decision Making," *Harvard Business Review*, Sept.-Oct. 1998, pp. 47–58.
3. K. Popper, *The Logic of Scientific Discovery* (New York: Basic Books, 1959), *Conjectures and Refutations* (New York: Basic Books, 1962), and *Realism and the Aim of Science* (London: Routledge, 2001).
4. T. Davenport and J. Harris, *Competing on Analytics* (Boston: Harvard Business School Press, 2007), p. 30.
5. Davenport and Harris, *Competing on Analytics*, p. 42.
6. M. May, *The Elegant Solution* (New York: Free Press, 2006).
7. More precisely, he refers back to Toyoda's principle of "the pursuit of perfection."
8. Author interview with R. Valenstein, Mar. 7, 2007.
9. Charles Fishman calls it the "presumption of imperfection" in an article that's noteworthy for his comparison of Toyota's Georgetown, Kentucky, factory to a brain focused not on making cars but on making better ways to make cars. C. Fishman, "No Satisfaction at Toyota," *Fast Company*, Dec. 2006, p. 82.
10. This is information theory's concept of mutual information, which is the amount of information that a variable like an indicator can provide about and a variable like the choice

among competing assumptions. The last section of the chapter expands on the idea.

11. You can assume the average daily customer rate jumps around from month to month for this store because I stipulated that the indicator could not overturn an assumption about kimono effectiveness in drawing customers. That means it wouldn't be so shocking if the kimono were successfully offsetting some negative factor.

12. Bayes' theorem states: $p(h/e) = p(h) \times (p(e/h)/p(e))$ where $p(a)$ means the probability of a and $p(a/b)$ means the probability of a if b is true.

13. Information theory defines these concepts as entropy. The entropy H of an indicator e is the average surprise or improbability of results e_i: $H(e_i) = -\Sigma_i p(e_i) \times \log_2 p(e_i)$. See T. Cover and J. Thomas, *Elements of Information Theory* (Hoboken, N.J.: Wiley, 1991).

14. The relevance $R(e,h_i)$ of result e to a set of assumptions h_i is given by: $R(e,h_i) = \Sigma_i p(h_i/e) \times \log_2 p(e/h_i)$ where $p(a/b)$ is the probability of a if b is true. The relevance $R(e_i,h_j)$ of indicator e_i to assumptions h_j is given by the expected value of the relevance of each result to the assumptions, a concept that information theorists define as conditional entropy: $R(e_i,h_j) = H(e_i/h_j) = -\Sigma_{ij} p(e_i \& h_j) \times \log_2 p(e_i/h_j)$. See Cover and Thomas, *Elements of Information Theory*, p. 16.

Chapter Five

1. S. Berinato, "What Went Wrong at Cisco," *CIO*, Aug. 1, 2001, pp. 52–58.

2. Berinato, "What Went Wrong at Cisco," p. 54.

3. Berinato, "What Went Wrong at Cisco," p. 56. The original comment was reported in the *Financial Times*.

4. Author interview with B. Bien, Mar. 30, 2007.

5. Energy companies are most advanced in their approach to performance management. Shell, Valero, and Koch Industries have been especially innovative.

6. The simplest definition of economic profit is operating profit less the risk-adjusted cost of capital. It's usually measured on an after-tax basis. What's hard is estimating that risk-adjusted cost. One way is to estimate the risk premium above the risk-free rate of return that pure-play companies comparable to your operations pay to their investors on all of their financing and then scale that premium to your operations using revenue. The Modigliani-Miller theorem, which asserts that the value of a firm is independent of its capital structure, lets you do this without regard to differences in how you and the comparable companies finance operations.

7. To my knowledge, Shell was the first to split controllable and uncontrollable causes of performance surprises.

8. D. Davidson, *Subjective, Intersubjective, Objective* (Oxford: Clarendon Press, 2001), p. 213.

9. On the other hand, you needed both a set of projections and a set of actual results to define the overall performance surprise, just as you need to slice a freshly baked pie twice to extract the first piece.

10. J. Collins, *From Good to Great* (New York: HarperBusiness, 2001), p. 104.

11. Collins, *From Good to Great*, pp. 106–107.

12. The example is mine, but the thinking leans heavily on the work of Donald Davidson, to whom I've given nods for related work in this chapter and Chapter Two. See Donald Davidson, *Inquiries into Truth and Meaning* (Oxford: Clarendon Press, 2001).

13. S. J. Gould, "Capturing the Center,"*Natural History*, 1998, *107*, 18.

14. Boeing acquired McDonnell Douglas in 1997, Daimler-Benz acquired Chrysler in 1998, and K-Mart acquired Sears in 2005.

15. *Defense Daily*, Sept. 27, 1994. Stonecipher later succeeded Phil Condit as CEO of Boeing but resigned within two years due to a personal relationship, violating the firm's code of conduct, with government relations executive Debra Peabody.

16. D. Smith and M. Sorge, "Chrysler's Bob Eaton—He's Sure No Shy Guy," *Ward's Auto World*, July 1992, p. 28.
17. Business Biographies, retrieved Apr. 11, 2007, from www.answers.com/alan+lacy?cat=biz-fin.

Chapter Six

1. This is nothing more than the standard deviation of the gaps around a trend line. If you need to, you can define it more precisely as the square root of the expected value of the square of the difference between actual gaps and their average or trend line predictions.
2. Since these are standard deviations and may covary, the numbers need not add up.
3. The exception is continuous process improvement programs that have begun to divide root causes of defects into controllable factors, uncontrollable factors, and process design errors.
4. Thanks to the Corporate Executive Board's Scott Bohannon for recognizing and crystallizing this challenge in carrying out the analysis.
5. "Ten Reasons for Investing in Nestlé," *Equity Note* (Bank Sarasin & Co. Ltd.), Jan. 8, 2007, p. 2.
6. Suzy Wetlaufer, "The Business Case Against Revolution: An Interview with Nestlé's Peter Brabeck," *Harvard Business Review*, Feb. 2001, p. 113.
7. Author interview with Jean-Daniel Luthi, May 22, 2007.
8. C. Busco and others, "Integrating Global Organizations Through Performance Measurement Systems," *Strategic Finance*, 2006, 87, 31–35.
9. Transfer prices between strategic business units producing products and zones distributing them are also to some extent negotiable, ensuring that errors in those prices do not bias the negotiation of specific targets.
10. Wetlaufer, "The Business Case Against Revolution."

11. More precisely, the market sets a relation between the excess returns on investment and the amount of risk correlated with the overall market's risk.

Conclusion

1. Sheldon Bell, CFO of Purolator Courier Ltd. A subsequent exchange with him on June 20, 2007, suggests this goes both ways. Operating manager requests for finance to track new indicators for which no forecasts exist may complicate performance analysis. But reviews of performance results without up-to-date forecasts also risk rehashing old news about outdated budget plans.

Acknowledgments

Well over a hundred general managers and financial executives have had an impact on this book through the innovative ways they've simplified the problem their organizations face of learning from experience despite masses of conflicting information. Since this book tries to shape dozens of these ideas into a coherent framework, it's impossible to do justice to their authors. Here I'll have to content myself with thanking some of the people most directly involved in the research.

Robert Kaplan and David Norton deserve thanks for putting together a performance management framework in the form of their balanced scorecard that's rich enough to support the extended criticism this book proposes of some of the ways organizations use it. Nestlé's Jean-Daniel Luthi, Toyota's Rich Valenstein, former GE managers Gino Picasso and Randy Drummond, and Purolator's Sheldon Bell provided illuminating interviews and comments. Neil Gaskell and Eric Dunn, both friends who have become private equity pirates, kindly read and commented on the manuscript in its entirety. To the extent it manages to reflect those comments, it's a much better book. Walter Greenblatt helped me crystallize the premise after I finished writing *Risk Intelligence*.

A number of people involved in that earlier and narrower book had an impact that is also strongly felt in this one. Stephen Altschul, a pioneer in the use of mutual information to sequence genes, helped me align that concept with this book's approach to valuing information. My *Risk* editor, Kirsten Sandberg, and Gail Ross Literary agent Howard Yoon tirelessly clarified the general argument. Joe Firestone strengthened it through patient criticism. And Jossey-Bass's Rebecca Browning added a crucial final coherency check of the draft manuscript.

Many colleagues provided direct and indirect support at the Corporate Executive Board, an international problem-solving network of business executives that seems to get hold of all the good strategic ideas at some point. Scott Bohannon not only helped shape a role that let me pursue independent research but provided substantive support by testing and extending the ideas. Kurt Reisenberg balanced my responsibilities to keep me in touch with research teams pursuing creative projects that constantly challenged the thinking on these pages. Among the research managers who contributed to that thinking are John Roberts, Anil Prahlad, Avi Alpert, Bernie Fallon, Marc Austin, Roisin Ryan, Jo Robinson, Jason van Tassel, and Mark Wiedemer. Mike Griffin, Sampriti Ganguli, and Eisha Armstrong provided further management cover besides the friendship for which I'm most grateful. Darren Howell, now at Citicorp, provided useful insight into problem solving at Capital One. Anita Feidler helped me track down a few documents locked stubbornly behind Web site passwords. And my good friend and *Globalist* editor Stephan Richter let me forge an early application of the argument in the crucible of a general readership article.

The Author

David Apgar is a director for investment and risk strategy at BlueOrchard Finance, the oldest of the for-profit microfinance funds, and a managing director at the Corporate Executive Board, where he launched best practices research programs for corporate controllers and treasurers between 2001 and 2003. He joined the board in 1998 from McKinsey, where he served insurance, reinsurance, and capital markets clients as a consultant and an engagement manager for three years. Prior to that, he was responsible for numerous finance company, bank, and insurer mergers and acquisitions assignments as a vice president in Lehman Brothers' Financial Institutions Group, and for building a framework for bank security sales as senior policy adviser to the comptroller of the currency. He proposed a debt relief program for Mexico and designed the precursor to interest rate relief Brady bonds as staff economist to Senator Bill Bradley.

Apgar holds an A.B. from Harvard, an M.A. from Oxford, and a Ph.D. from the Rand Graduate School. He occasionally teaches risk management and international development at Johns Hopkins School of Advanced International Studies. He is the author of *Risk Intelligence: Learning to Manage What We Don't Know* (2006).

Index